LETTERS FROM
IWO JIMA

昭
和
19
年
11
月
28
日
沼
津

栗
林
忠
道

お略　私は相変らず無事ですから御安心下さい

十月三日付、十月二十日付（二通）十月二十七日に

どうした訳か大変遅れて十月十日頃着いた

より後にやつと着いた訳です

十月二十日付のものには本日十才の近...つた手紙と対

何れも紅葉を送りくれ...

吉田さんの所へ行ったとの話せ...外出され

しかしいくら思っても...お手上げ手紙を待つ命です

中隊飛び...いたい時のみたい時...

寒い雨だって...しのぐが何...

......

それより...

......

何卒宜しく...

......

......

......

......

......

......

大和にやらせて下さい上国の様に...すればよかろう）と思ふ

LETTERS FROM
IWO JIMA

—

*The Japanese eyewitness stories
that inspired Clint Eastwood's film*

KUMIKO KAKEHASHI

Weidenfeld & Nicolson

LONDON

First published in Great Britain in 2007
by Weidenfeld & Nicolson

3 5 7 9 10 8 6 4 2

Translation copyright © 2007 by Shinochosha Co., Ltd

Originally published in Japan as *Chipuẓo Kanashiki* by Shinchosha Co.,
Ltd., Tokyo, copyright © 2005 Kukimo Kakehashi.

A CIP catalogue record for this book
is available from the British Library.

All photographs, except those on page 6 on insert are courtesy of
Fumiko Kuribayashi.
Photograph on page 6 copyright © Tsunetaka Shishikura

Map © Jmap

hardback ISBN: 978 0 297 85332 9
export trade paperback ISBN: 978 0 297 85333 6

Printed in Great Britain by Mackays of Chatham plc, Chatham, Kent

Weidenfeld & Nicolson

The Orion Publishing Group Ltd
Orion House
5 Upper Saint Martin's Lane
London, WC2H 9EA

www.orionbooks.co.uk

CONTENTS

MAP OF IWO JIMA

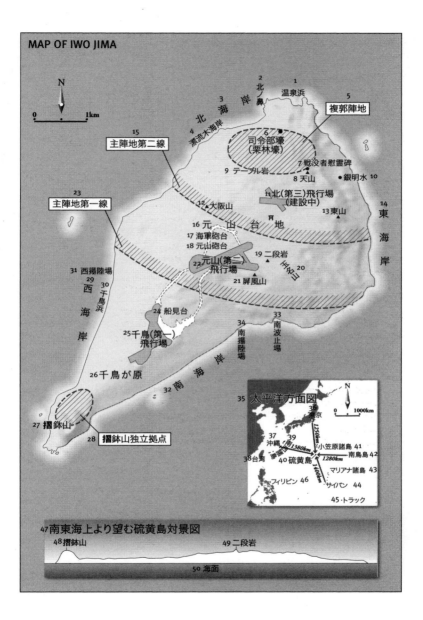

N

0   1km

2 北ノ鼻　1 温泉浜

5

複郭陣地

3 北海岸

4 漂流木海岸

15 主陣地第二線

司令部壕
（栗林壕）

6 7 戦没者慰霊碑

9 テーブル岩　8 天山　●銀明水 10

11 北（第三）飛行場
（建設中）

12 ▲大阪山　13 東山

14 東海岸

23 主陣地第一線

16 元　山　台　地

17 海軍砲台
18 元山砲台

19 ▲二段岩

22 元山（第二）飛行場

旭　日　原 20

21 屏風山

31 西揚陸場

30 千鳥浜

29

西海岸

24 船見台

25 千鳥（第一）飛行場

34 南揚陸場

33 南波止場

26 千鳥が原

32 南　海　岸

27 摺鉢山

28 摺鉢山独立拠点

35 太平洋方面図

N

0   1000km

39 東京

36

37 沖縄

38 台湾

39

小笠原諸島 41

南鳥島 42

40 硫黄島

マリアナ諸島 43

サイパン 44

フィリピン 46

45・トラック

1250km
1380km
1280km
1100km

47 南東海上より望む硫黄島対景図

48 摺鉢山　　49 二段岩

50 海面

PROLOGUE

He had been very talkative up to that point, but when we got to the subject of the telegram, he went quiet for a moment. Then, snapping to attention, he began to intone in a voice so firm that it belied his eighty-five years: "The battle is entering its final chapter. Since the enemy's landing, the gallant fighting of the men under my command has been such that even the gods would weep."

The peaceful sun was pouring into the living room of the cramped house where the old couple—he was eighty-five, she seventy-five—lived in Nangoku in Kôchi Prefecture. On the comfortable, old-fashioned sofa sat an unopened box containing a robot dog that their grandchild had sent them from Tokyo as a substitute pet. "How can I possibly be expected to make head or tail of the instruction manual at my age?" the old man grumbled just a minute ago. Now, his voice quite transformed, he continued:

> In particular, I humbly rejoice in the fact that they have con-
> tinued to fight bravely though utterly empty-handed and ill-
> equipped against a land, sea, and air attack of a material
> superiority that surpasses the imagination.
> One after another they are falling to the ceaseless and fero-
> cious attacks of the enemy. For this reason, the situation has
> arisen whereby I must disappoint your expectations and yield
> this important place to the hands of the enemy. With humility
> and sincerity, I offer my repeated apologies.

Our ammunition is gone and our water dried up. Now is
the time for us all to make the final counterattack and fight gallantly . . .

His voice was growing a little hoarse, and the unexpected recitation
came to an abrupt end.

The expression on his face now back to normal, he looked at me and
smiled as if slightly embarrassed. Then, his expression serious once
more, he said: "For me that message is like a sutra. It was the last message his lordship left us. It still just comes out word perfect like that. I
can't forget a single word of it."

The man Sadaoka Nobuyoshi was referring to as "his lordship" was
none other than Lieutenant General Kuribayashi Tadamichi, commander in chief of Iwo Jima, the scene of some of the most savage fighting of the Pacific War. With a force of a little over twenty thousand
men, Kuribayashi waged a campaign of unprecedented bloodshed and
endurance.

Meticulous and rational in the way he fought, Kuribayashi inflicted
enormous damage on the Americans after they landed before eventually switching to guerrilla tactics. Ultimately, Iwo Jima, which was
thought likely to fall in five days, ended up holding out for thirty-six.

What Sadaoka Nobuyoshi had recited were the opening lines of the
farewell telegram Lieutenant General Kuribayashi dispatched to the
Imperial General Headquarters on March 16, 1945, when defeat and
death were staring him in the face.

Within the American military, the marines had a reputation as a
wild bunch of toughs, but even for them Iwo Jima was a gruesome and
terrifying battle variously described as *the worst battle in history* and a
hell within hell. Confronted with his own imminent death, the commander in chief had composed his final dispatch in an attempt to let the
world know how bravely his men had fought and died on that isolated
island 1,250 kilometers south of Tokyo, so far away from home.

The battle of Iwo Jima was hopeless from the start.

A cursory look at the discrepancy in fighting power between the two sides makes clear that the Japanese did not stand a one-in-ten-thousand chance of winning. The Japanese force on the island had neither airplanes nor warships to support them.

The same was true for land-based fighting power. Against a Japanese force of around twenty thousand men, some sixty thousand American troops came ashore, and backing up those sixty thousand were a further one hundred thousand support troops. The defeat and destruction of the Japanese forces was self-evident; their only real aim was to hold out for as long as they could in an effort to delay the American invasion of the Japanese homeland.

Against such a background, Kuribayashi wanted to take the last chance he had to tell the world how his men—most of them conscripts in their thirties or older, many of whom had left wives and children at home to come to the front—had fought so brave and yet so tragic a fight that "even the gods would weep"—a Japanese expression meaning that neither the souls of the dead nor the gods of heaven or of earth would be able to remain unmoved.

Sadaoka was not one of those men.

"I wanted to die together with his lordship." Who knows how desperately he wanted that fate as a young man of twenty-six? But it was not to be.

Sadaoka was not a soldier but a civilian working for the military. In other words, he worked for the army, but fighting was not one of his duties.

In 1941, three and a half years before the fall of Iwo Jima, Kuribayashi was chief of staff of the South China Expeditionary Force (23rd Army) in Canton (present-day Guangzhou in China), while Sadaoka was working in the "tailoring section" responsible for mending the clothing of the officers.

One day, another civilian employee who worked in administration under Kuribayashi came over. "The chief of staff wants me to ask if any of you can make him a white shirt," he said. The tailoring section dealt with army uniforms, and most of what they did was mending. There was nobody able to tailor a dress shirt.

But Sadaoka dismantled a shirt he had brought with him from Japan and examined how it was put together. "I can do it," he volunteered. Now he was able to go in and out of Kuribayashi's private rooms, and Kuribayashi spoke to him kindly.

The difference in their relative stations was as wide as the gulf between heaven and earth. Kuribayashi was an officer in his early fifties, while Sadaoka was in his twenties and a mere tailor. But Kuribayashi was genuinely fond of the young man. Sadaoka came from the Shikoku countryside. He had earned good grades at school, but his family was not in an economic position to send him on to college, so he had applied for the South China Expeditionary Force because he wanted to "get over to the continent and see the world."

IT WAS FEBRUARY 2004 when I visited Sadaoka in his home near Harimaya-bashi Bridge in the center of Kôchi—almost fifty-nine years after the defeat at Iwo Jima.

After my interest in Kuribayashi had first been sparked, I found that the more research I did, the more I was drawn to the man. When a member of the Kuribayashi family told me that a onetime civilian employee of the military who had had a special bond with Kuribayashi was still alive and well, I lost no time in getting in touch.

"If you are an admirer of his lordship, then you are family as far as I'm concerned."

As Sadaoka welcomed me with these words, he brought out a photograph. It was from 1943, he said, and had been taken in the barracks of the South China Expeditionary Force in Canton.

The picture was of the garden of the barracks. Kuribayashi in his uniform and his boots was sitting on a chair with a white seat cover, his sword in his hand. Beside him was a military dog, a German shepherd, and behind him stood five men, one of whom was the young Sadaoka.

"When they decided to have the picture taken, his lordship said, 'This is too good an opportunity to miss. Let's call Sadaoka,' and he sent a messenger to fetch me. I was in my quarters inside the base, but to get from the garden where the photograph was taken to my quarters and back took a good fifteen minutes, even if you ran at full tilt. His lordship was good enough to wait for me all that time."

Under normal circumstances it was quite unthinkable that an army officer should wait fifteen entire minutes for a mere tailor. But I imagine that Kuribayashi wanted to give Sadaoka, a country boy, the chance to have his photo taken, which was still something rare and exotic at the time. In the picture, Sadaoka is standing very upright and stiff directly behind Kuribayashi with a rather tense expression on his face.

The army was an institution where social class distinctions were carried to an extreme, and for Kuribayashi to be so open and friendly with his "inferiors" made him a most unusual officer. When soldiers were hospitalized, he would personally drive over to visit them in the military hospital, bearing gifts of fruit. He also delivered soothing ice to soldiers who suffered from malaria.

Sadaoka, who frequently accompanied Kuribayashi, said to him one day half in jest, "When they get a visit from you in person, the patients probably feel so embarrassed that they can't sleep peacefully."

Kuribayashi only smiled at the time, but starting with their next visit, he parked the car outside the hospital gates and would send Sadaoka in to visit the sick men on his behalf while he waited outside.

Sadaoka loved this man, Kuribayashi, more than his true father, and when Kuribayashi was promoted to lieutenant general and transferred to the Second Imperial Guards Home Division in Tokyo in June 1943, Sadaoka put in a request for a transfer and remained with him.

But a year later, when it was decided that Kuribayashi was to be sent to Iwo Jima as commander in chief, he forbade Sadaoka to go with him.

Sadaoka was in torment. In August, two months after Kuribayashi had departed for Iwo Jima, he boarded a ship bound for Chichi Jima, around 270 kilometers north of Iwo Jima, "in pursuit of his lordship." Iwo Jima is located almost at the southernmost tip of the Ogasawara Islands, but politically it is part of Metropolitan Tokyo. It was Chichi Jima, however, that was the political and economic center of the Ogasawara Islands, and transport ships plied between there and the mainland.

Determined to be reunited with Kuribayashi, Sadaoka spent a whole night walking from Tokyo to Yokohama. After he had waited a week at the port, he came across a boat going to Chichi Jima.

"I am a civilian employee of Lieutenant General Kuribayashi. I want you to take me to his lordship," he announced as he forced his way on board.

"Papers and written permissions? I had nothing like that with me. Frankly, I've got no idea why they let me on board. Maybe it was just that the war was turning against us and I was able to take advantage of the general confusion to sneak on."

Once Sadaoka got to Chichi Jima and finally managed to get through to talk to Kuribayashi on the radio telephone, he was subjected to a stinging rebuke. "What the hell do you think you're doing there?" bellowed Kuribayashi. "I categorically forbid you to come out to this island."

"It was the only time his lordship had ever shouted at me—the only time."

Sadaoka's eyes swam with tears as he told me that he never heard Kuribayashi's voice again.

He stayed in Chichi Jima until December of that year. Kuribayashi talked about Sadaoka in the letters he wrote to his wife, Yoshii, back in Tokyo. On December 11, 1944, he wrote:

I heard that Sadaoka will be returning to the mainland on the next ship. He took the trouble to come all this way but was unable to see me. To top it off, he got sick and had to go into hospital, and that's what finally persuaded him to go home. When he gets back to Tokyo he's sure to drop in on the house. When he does, don't just keep him out in the entrance hall, but please go out of your way to be nice to him. I heard that he's eventually planning to go back to his hometown in the country.

Kuribayashi had driven Sadaoka off because he did not want him to die in vain for his sake, and he was obviously concerned about this young man who had followed him so far to the south. Kuribayashi again mentioned Sadaoka in another letter written only eleven days later, on December 22, 1944: "I think that after taking the trouble to come out here and then having to go back to Japan without seeing me, he'll probably end up returning to his hometown. That's what war is like for all of us, after all."

The expression "taking the trouble to come" appears for a second time. Clearly, Kuribayashi understood how Sadaoka, who had traveled so far in order to see him, felt toward him. His comment, "That's what war is like for all of us," is not so much stoic, soldierly resignation, but has a poignant ring as if he is admonishing himself.

After Sadaoka wrote to announce that he had reached Tokyo safely, Kuribayashi sent him a letter from Iwo Jima.

In reply to your esteemed letter:
Your card from Tokyo reached me. It is a pity that we could not meet here, but I am delighted that you returned safely. You mention that you were good enough to visit my house in Tokyo and I am deeply grateful for your kindness.
I am in the best of health and have continued to work hard as usual, so there is no need for concern in that regard. Farewell.

The letter is kind and warm—quite unlike the occasion when Kuribayashi shouted at him. In fact, the letter is so politely worded that you would never guess it was addressed to only a young civilian employee. It is written with neat brushstrokes on a postcard printed with the words "Army Post." Yellowed now with the passage of almost sixty years, the postcard is carefully stored away in a safe in Sadaoka's house.

This message was sent at the end of December 1944, when the air attacks and the naval barrage against Iwo Jima were growing ever more intense. The Americans landed less than two months later, on February 19, 1945, and Kuribayashi is thought to have died in battle at dawn on March 26.

Sadaoka was finally able to get to Iwo Jima in 1978, thirty-three years after Kuribayashi's death. Iwo Jima was occupied by the United States for twenty-three years after the war, and Japanese citizens could not visit the island until after it was returned to Japan in 1968.

Sadaoka went to the island with a group on a memorial pilgrimage, and when the guide pointed out the command bunker where Kuribayashi is believed to have been based, he could not stop himself from rushing toward it.

"It's me, your lordship. It's me, Sadaoka," he shouted at the top of his voice. "Here I am at last."

A FEW DAYS AFTER I got back to Tokyo from Kôchi, I was in the library looking through newspaper articles from 1945 about the defeat at Iwo Jima, when I almost gasped aloud with surprise.

It was the *Asahi Shimbun* newspaper of March 22, 1945. On the front page was a large headline that read: "Iwo Jima Falls to the Enemy: Heroic Commander in Chief Stands at the Head of His Forces: All-Out Attack." The article included Kuribayashi's farewell telegram in its entirety, but it was different from what Sadaoka had recited from memory that day.

> The battle is entering its final chapter. At midnight on the seventeenth, I will stand at the head of my men, and, praying for the certain victory and the security of the Imperial fatherland, all of us will resolutely carry out a heroic all-out attack.

I pulled out my notebook and checked my transcription of the telegram as Sadaoka had recited it to me. It began: "The battle is entering its final chapter. Since the enemy's landing, the gallant fighting of the men under my command has been such that even the gods would weep."

I was right. It was totally different.

Sadaoka looked the picture of robust health, but he was, after all, eighty-five years old. It wouldn't be strange if his memory had played a trick on him. But when I remembered the resonant voice in which he had intoned the dispatch, I changed my mind: it wasn't possible. After all, how could he possibly make a mistake about the last words of "his lordship"?

I had a sudden thought, and started looking for a book I was sure the library would have. It was the *Senshisôsho,* a series on the history of the war compiled by the Military History Department of the National Institute for Defense Studies in the postwar years. Regarded as the most detailed and objective record of the war, it is the so-called official published history. If the correct text of Kuribayashi's farewell message was anywhere, it would be there.

And sure enough, there it was, on page 410 in volume thirteen of the sixty-eight volumes on the army: *Chûbu Taiheyô Rikugun Sakusen 2 Periryû• Angauru• Iô-Jima* ("*Mid-Pacific Army Operations 2: Peleliu, Angaur, Iwo Jima*"): "The battle is entering its final chapter. Since the enemy's landing, the gallant fighting of the men under my command has been such that even the gods would weep. . . ."

Sadaoka had not been wrong. What he had recited from memory that day had been almost perfectly correct. I then checked all the books written about Iwo Jima. Many of them quoted Kuribayashi's farewell telegram, but in every case the text they used was the same as in the official published history. Perhaps Sadaoka had gotten his version from one of the books.

That had to mean that the text published in the newspapers had been altered.

But surely Kuribayashi, who had held Iwo Jima for over a month in the face of a ferocious American assault, was highly regarded by the military leadership? On the night of March 21, the prime minister, Kuniaki Koiso, made a speech on the radio about the last stand on Iwo Jima in which he praised Kuribayashi and the defense garrison for their "heroic resistance," which was the "culmination of the Japanese spirit."

Kuribayashi was also popular among the ordinary people. While few may know his name now, on countless occasions when I've asked people from the generation that lived through that time what they know about Iwo Jima, they instantly reply, "the great general Kuribayashi."

So why then should there be any need to change the last words of such a famous man? Let's compare both versions. First of all, here is Kuribayashi's original message.

The battle is entering its final chapter. Since the enemy's landing, the gallant fighting of the men under my command has been such that even the gods would weep. In particular, I humbly rejoice in the fact that they have continued to fight bravely though *utterly empty-handed and ill-equipped* against a land, sea, and air attack of a material superiority such as surpasses the imagination.

One after another they are falling in the ceaseless and ferocious attacks of the enemy. For this reason, the situation has arisen whereby I must disappoint your expectations and yield this important place to the hands of the enemy. With humility and sincerity, I offer my repeated apologies.

Our ammunition is gone and our water dried up. Now is the time for us all to make the final counterattack and fight gallantly, conscious of the Emperor's favor, not begrudging our efforts though they turn our bones to powder and pulverize our bodies.

I believe that until this island is recaptured, the Emperor's domain will be eternally insecure. I therefore swear that even when I have become a ghost I shall look forward to turning the defeat of the Imperial Army into victory.

I stand now at the beginning of the end. At the same time as revealing my inmost feelings, I pray earnestly for the unfailing victory and the security of the Empire. Farewell for all eternity.

I then looked at the text as published in the newspaper.

The battle is entering its final chapter. At midnight on the seventeenth, I will stand at the head of my men, and, praying for the certain victory and the security of the Imperial fatherland, *all of us will resolutely carry out a heroic all-out attack.*

I humbly rejoice in the fact that they have continued to fight bravely, since the enemy's landing, against the enemy's land, sea, and air attack of a material superiority such as surpasses the imagination, and the gallant fighting of the men under my command has been such that even the gods would weep.

One after another the officers and men are falling in the ceaseless and ferocious attacks of the enemy. For this reason, the situation has arisen whereby I must disappoint your expectations, and am forced to yield this important place to the hands of the enemy. With humility and sincerity, I offer my repeated apologies.

I believe that until this island is recaptured, the Emperor's domain will be eternally insecure. I therefore swear that even when I have become a ghost I shall look forward to turning the defeat of the Imperial Army into victory. Our ammunition is gone and our water dried up. Now is the time for all the survivors to make the final counterattack and fight gallantly, conscious of the Emperor's graciousness, not begrudging our efforts though they turn our bones to powder and pulverize our bodies.

At this point *I together with all my officers and men reverently chanting banzais for the Emperor's long life* bid you farewell for all eternity. [Emphasis added.]

So how do the two versions differ?

In Kuribayashi's original text, the first thing he talks about is the bravery of his men. By contrast, the altered text that was published in the newspapers emphasizes "the certain victory and the security of the Imperial fatherland," rather than the soldiers themselves. Equally, the words "heroic all-out attack"—a commonly used expression at the time that served as a stock euphemism to beautify final suicide charges—do not appear in Kuribayashi's message.

There are no major changes in the fifth paragraph of the text, except for the insertion of one phrase that does not appear in Kuribayashi's original: "I together with all my officers and men reverently chanting banzais for the Emperor's long life."

There is one section, however, that has been cut from the newspaper in its entirety: the part about being "utterly empty-handed and ill-equipped."

The agony and the frustration of soldiers who had to keep on fighting when they had no weapons and their supplies had been cut off—that is probably what Kuribayashi wanted to get across most desperately. And it is this part that has been excised.

Talking about being "empty-handed and ill-equipped" is tantamount to whining. A proper soldier never complains, no matter how hard things get, but sticks it out, keeps on fighting, and goes to his death in silence. The accepted "common sense" of the time comes through in this change.

Kuribayashi's own text does include some of the stock phrases used by military men of the time—for example, "conscious of the Emperor's favor, not begrudging our efforts though they turn our bones to powder and pulverize our bodies," and "turning the defeat of the Imperial Army into victory"—so in terms of style it conformed to the formal conventions of a commander in chief's farewell telegram. But at the same time it conjures up a vivid image of the doomed and dying soldiers having to face an overwhelmingly more powerful enemy "empty-handed and ill-equipped," with their "ammunition gone" and their "water dried up." What permeates the whole message is the raw grief of the commander summarized neatly in the phrase "such that even the gods would weep."

It was this, I suspect, that alarmed the upper echelons of the military establishment.

Farewell telegrams were always sent to the Imperial General Headquarters, but they were also published in the newspapers to be read by the general public. Kuribayashi must have been aware of that. He was making an effort to communicate the heroism of his men not just to the Imperial General Headquarters, but more widely to the man in the street. High-ranking army officials, however, decided that publishing the text in the newspapers in its original form might give offense.

Right next to the article on the defeat at Iwo Jima, on the front page of that day's *Asahi Shimbun* newspaper, is an article about the proposal of a special military measures bill in the legislature (National Diet). The bill gave the government the legal power to expropriate land and buildings, force individuals to perform certain necessary duties, and get unconditional cooperation from corporations in the event of a final battle against the Americans on the Japanese mainland.

At a time when Prime Minister Koiso was making speeches about "the only choice we have" being "between victory and death" and urging "one hundred million fellow countrymen . . . to fight together with the army, should the enemy come, and exterminate them completely," it was hardly surprising that Kuribayashi's message was deemed likely to undermine the morale of the people.

Kuribayashi, who had thought about becoming a journalist in his youth, wrote a letter to his wife on January 21, 1945, from Iwo Jima saying: "It's best that you say as little as you can to newspaper journalists or anyone else like that. You must be especially careful if they ask you to show them any letters. If you're thoughtless and end up showing them anything, it's guaranteed it will be in the paper in no time." Clearly, he was conscious of how he would be treated by the newspapers and other media. The last letter he wrote to his elder brother, Yoshima, on January 12, 1945, includes the following passage.

> *Perhaps I'm just worrying needlessly, but there is a general tendency for newspapers and magazines to cook up articles that have no basis in truth about how notable people got where they are in life. As an example, take the story that as a boy General Ugaki put himself through school by selling daikon radishes or delivering newspapers. It's simply not the truth. These are just stories that journalists have cobbled together by distorting and exaggerating things irresponsibly.*
>
> *As a boy, I was raised in the house where I was born. I then went to Nagano Middle School, progressed smoothly through the Military Academy and the Army War College, and got where I am today with help from my seniors and other people. I sincerely hope I have done nothing that could embarrass me after my death.*

Despite the atmosphere in Japan in those days, Kuribayashi was able to take a cool, detached look at the way he would be placed on a pedestal after his death as "a commander in chief who had died with honor." He knew perfectly well that the text of his farewell telegram would be published in the newspapers—and that was why he wrote what he did.

He added a *jisei*—a death poem in three stanzas—to the end of the farewell telegram.

> *Unable to complete this heavy task for our country*
> *Arrows and bullets all spent, so sad we fall.*
>
> *But unless I smite the enemy,*
> *My body cannot rot in the field.*
> *Yea, I shall be born again seven times*
> *And grasp the sword in my hand.*
>
> *When ugly weeds cover this island,*
> *My sole thought shall be the Imperial Land.*

In their death poems, soldiers of the Imperial Army were traditionally expected to write about love of country and devotion to the emperor. In Kuribayashi's poem, for example, the idea in lines 5–6—"Yea, I shall be born again seven times / And grasp the sword in my hand"— is derived from *"Shichishôhôkoku,"* a stock phrase of the time that means "to be reborn seven times to serve one's country." The case can be made that Kuribayashi's poem contains all the proper clichés that a death poem composed by the commander of a defeated army should.

But here, too, there is something different. Something we must not overlook.

"So sad we fall"—the end of the first line in the Japanese poem—is changed in the newspaper version to "mortified, we fall."

Kuribayashi wrote that soldiers were "sad" to die for their country.

Undoubtedly, he was giving honest expression to his most acute feelings, but that was not acceptable in the middle of a war on which the fate of the nation was riding.

The next day, I went to visit Kuribayashi's family and got them to show me the real thing.

Kuribayashi's farewell telegram had been sent to the Imperial General Headquarters, but after his death, Colonel Tanemura Sakô of the Army General Staff, who headed the Twentieth Army Corps, visited Kuribayashi's home and presented the telegram to his wife, Yoshii, with the words: "Regard this telegram as the sacred bones of your dead husband." From the general all the way down to the common soldier, Iwo Jima was a battleground from which the bones of none of the dead made it home.

The message was three pages long and was written in the hand of the telegraph operator who had received it. The three stanzas of the death poem were on the final page.

There was a red mark in the shape of two concentric circles at the head of the very first line—the line that had been altered. Then the word "sad" had been blocked out with a thick black line, and the word "mortified" had been written in its place. Both the black of the crossing out and the red of the circles looked fresh, bright, and new.

In this telegram there was no sign that the body of the text had been tampered with. The main text was probably "reworked" when it was published in the newspaper. The detail that caught the attention of the Imperial General Headquarters and that they felt they could not leave unchanged was the word "sad" in the death poem.

Sadaoka had told me that Kuribayashi's farewell message was "like a sutra" for him. At the time, I had interpreted it to mean that he chanted the text whenever he thought of Kuribayashi in order to soothe his ghost. But when I compared the original version with the doctored version that appeared in the newspaper, the farewell message that I had originally thought of as having a quintessentially soldierly beauty revealed a whole new side of Kuribayashi to me.

This telegram was an ode for the repose of the souls of the soldiers who had already died or were about to die. Sadaoka had been frustrated in his attempt to die at Kuribayashi's side, but when he chanted the text he was performing an act of mourning for Kuribayashi's twenty thousand men in the commander in chief's place.

That was what Sadaoka had meant by the word "sutra."

AT THAT TIME I did not yet understand. I did not yet realize how much of a taboo it was for a Japanese commander to describe his soldiers as "sad" to go to their deaths. Kuribayashi was one of the officer elite. What did he experience on the battleground of Iwo Jima that drove him to write not only a poem, but a subtle protest against the military command that so casually sent men out to die?

LETTERS FROM
IWO JIMA

CHAPTER ONE

LEAVING FOR THE FRONT

—

Lᴇᴜᴛᴇɴᴀɴᴛ Gᴇɴᴇʀᴀʟ Kᴜʀɪʙᴀʏᴀsʜɪ Tᴀᴅᴀᴍɪᴄʜɪ sᴇᴛ ᴏғғ ғᴏʀ Iᴡᴏ Jima on June 8, 1944. His family was not informed of his destination. Whether you were a career soldier like Kuribayashi or just a conscript, in those days your family never knew to which theater of war you had been sent.

"This time maybe even my dead bones won't be sent back home," Kuribayashi told Yoshii, his wife. But he looked so relaxed that she did not take his remark seriously.

The final meal served at home that morning was herring wrapped in seaweed, and rice steamed with red beans. Yoshii had not boiled the red rice to celebrate her husband's departure for the front; she made it simply because it was one of his favorite dishes.

The Kuribayashis were a family of five. In addition to Tadamichi himself, there was his forty-year-old wife, Yoshii; Tarô, the eldest of the children and a young man of nineteen; a fifteen-year-old girl called Yôko; and finally another daughter, Takako, who, at nine, was the baby of the family. They lived in Tokyo, in a detached house not far from Higashi Matsubara on the Teito Line (now the Keiô Inokashira Line) to which they had moved less than two months earlier.

In September 1941, Kuribayashi had been appointed chief of staff of the South China Expeditionary Force (Twenty-third Army) in Canton and took part in the capture of Hong Kong in December of that year. In June 1943, he was made commander of the Second Imperial Guards Home Division, which was in charge of the defense of the capital, Tokyo. But he resigned this post in April 1944 to take responsibility for a subordinate who had accidentally started a fire, and was attached to the Eastern Army Headquarters. Obliged to leave the grand mansion he had lived in as division commander, he ended up renting the house in Higashi Matsubara.

Kuribayashi's de facto sinecure at the Eastern Army Headquarters did not last long. On May 27, he was given the command of the 109th Division. With a range of battlefield skills, the 109th was a large-scale force capable of carrying out independent operations.

The 109th had been created largely from units already in place on Chichi Jima in an effort to strengthen the defenses of the Ogasawara Islands. After his appointment as division commander, Kuribayashi had no time to relax in his new house but instead headed straight for Iwo Jima to take up his post.

His wife, Yoshii, and Takako saw him off.

Kuribayashi was shaving out on the veranda when Tarô left for school that morning. The farewell between father and son was low-key: "I'm off to school!" "All right, then."

Nine-year-old Takako was the one who worried Kuribayashi by bursting into tears. She was a student at Matsubara Elementary School, but it just so happened that, with school finishing early that day because of a parents' association meeting, she was back home in time to see her father off. Still, no one had the heart to scold the normally sensible and obedient girl for her moodiness.

The car came to the gate of the house to collect Kuribayashi in the early afternoon. Takako, who had no way of knowing that her father was setting off into the jaws of death, kept crying long after he had gone.

She sat down in the hall and wept for hours. The place was full of memories of her father. A stickler for punctuality, Kuriba-yashi would be ready to leave the house early every morning. He was in the habit of waiting in the hall for the adjutant who came to pick him up by car. During this short wait, he would ask his youngest daughter, herself about to head out to school, to dance for him. Takako, who was later to make her debut as a starlet of the Daiei film studio, would use the hallway step as a stage and de-light her father by singing "Ame-furi O-Tsuki-san" ("The Moon in the Rain") while mimicking traditional Japanese dance mo-tions.

On June 25, 1944, he sent Takako this letter.

My dear Tako-chan,

How are you, Tako-chan?

In my mind's eye, I can still see you and Mother standing by the gate to see me off on the day I left.

Since then, I've dreamed several times of going back home and taking a walk around the neighborhood with you and Mother. Sadly, though, it's something I can't really do.

You know, Tako-chan, Daddy just can't wait for you to grow up to be a support to your mother.

Build up your strength, study hard, and do exactly what your mother tells you to do. That will really put my mind at ease.

Now I must say "Good-bye."

Daddy at the front

Takako had been born when Kuribayashi was over forty years old. He doted on her, addressing her with the pet name of "Tako-chan," and generally made a fuss over her. She appeared frequently in her father's

dreams while he was at the front. On November 17, 1944, he wrote
to her:

Tako-chan! How are you? I'm fine!

*Last night we had two air raids: one just after I'd got to sleep and
another just as it was getting light. But I still managed to have a
funny dream.*

*In my dream, you, Tako-chan, had just got out of the bath and
were sniveling and whimpering. "Why are you crying?" I asked
you. "Was the bathwater too hot?" Then Mother appeared. She
laughed and said, "I bet it's because you want something nice and
sweet." Then she brought out her breast and put it in your mouth.
The two of you lay down, and your cheeks, Tako-chan, were all
puffed out as you sucked away greedily on the breast. You just
looked so very happy.*

*Just then out came your big sister. "I'm shocked!" she said. "I'm
shocked! Honestly, Tako-chan, still suckling at your age!" Then
she started poking your cheeks.*

*That was about all that happened, but Daddy saw all your faces
so clearly that it was just like being there with you.*

What do you think? A pretty funny dream, wasn't it?

Then, on December 23, 1944, he wrote:

*Tako-chan, a little while ago Daddy had another dream with
you in it.*

*In my dream, you were very tall—about as tall as me, in fact.
You also had on Daddy's pants, but your hair was in a bob.*

*I was marveling at how very tall you were, when, lo and behold,
who should turn up but your mother! With her there, I thought it*

would be nice if the two of us swung you between us the way we always did, but you were so very heavy we just couldn't do it!

Kuribayashi probably dreamed about Takako whimpering like a baby because he could not forget how she had cried when he had left for the front.

In his dream of the following month Takako was a grown-up. She was "tall" and "very heavy" and wore her father's hand-me-down pants, while her hair was done "in a bob"—just as when they parted at the gate. Outside of this dream, Kuribayashi was never to see Takako as an adult.

KURIBAYASHI WAS A PROLIFIC letter writer. In fact, it was a letter of his that I came across in a history of the war that first sparked my interest in him. Dated June 25, 1944—the same day he wrote his first letter to Takako—it was addressed to Yoshii, his wife.

The letter includes the phrase: "Please understand that I will not be sending you any more letters after this one," so Kuribayashi may well have intended it to serve as his final message before death. But the letter—seven pages in length—was totally atypical for the final message of a military man.

It starts by describing what the island looked like and the everyday lives of the men.

As regards water, there isn't any spring water here, so we just collect all the rainwater we can and make use of that. That's why I keep thinking how much I'd love a nice, cold drink of water, but there's absolutely no chance of that!

There are more mosquitoes and flies than I'd imagined. Most annoying. We have no newspapers, no wireless, and not a single shop. There's the odd farmer's house here and there, but they're only suitable for cows or horses. The men are all either living in tents or in caves. The caves are airless and humid, and they really are—really, truly—awful. I'm living the same way, too, naturally.

He then goes on to talk about an air raid on the island that occurred soon after he had taken up his post.

We have already had three air raids in which we were heavily bombed, hit with a rain of incendiary shells, and strafed with machine-gun fire. On the sixteenth, a massive bomb landed next to the dugout, setting off a huge explosion. I was convinced that the dugout—with me in it—would be blown to bits, but as luck would have it, I didn't even get a scratch. For the duration of the ferocious raid, the only thing I could do was wait in the dugout in a state of extreme anxiety, and pray.

By the time Kuribayashi arrived at his post in June, American air raids were taking a heavy toll. In three raids that month, the Japanese lost more than a hundred airplanes on the ground, while a raid on the sixteenth also killed forty soldiers. This sapped the morale of the Japanese forces and reinforced Kuribayashi's awareness of the acute challenges he faced. The Americans actually made their landing eight months later, but even in these early days the Japanese could not relax their guard for an instant.

"If the island I'm on is captured," wrote Kuribayashi in one of his letters, "the Japanese mainland will probably be subjected to air raids day and night." He urged his family to get out of Tokyo fast. The letter goes on: "Just when I thought that I, as both a husband and a father, was about to make a happy life for all of you, I have been ordered to defend the most crucial territory of all for Japan in this great war. It is a duty I have to accept."

He goes on to reveal his innermost thoughts:

Last of all, I want to say something to the children. Always do what your mother tells you. After I have gone, I want you to help your mother, treat her as the center of the family, and help each other so you can all live vigorous, positive lives. With you in particular Tarô, I pray with all my heart that you become the kind of strong, tough-minded young man that your mother and your younger sisters can depend on. Yôko, you are pretty robust, so I'm confident about you. I feel sorry for your mommy because maybe she hasn't got that strength of character. I do regret that I had so little time to love you, Tako-chan. Please grow up to be big and strong for me.

The letter certainly sounds like a final message.

After the concluding words, "Farewell to my wife and my children from your husband and your father," there is a three-part postscript:

1. By this post, I'm sending back anything I don't really need out of the things I brought over with me. I think they'll serve as keepsakes to remember me by (and it's possible that my possessions and my remains won't be delivered to you after I'm dead). Some military baggage may reach you, and I may send back more stuff later. Don't send me whiskey or any other extras like that. I really don't need them. Who knows if they'll get through to me, and even if they do, there's every chance I may no longer be alive by then anyway.

2. I think I more or less did everything that needed to be done around the house. I wanted to put something in to block the draft that comes up from under the kitchen floor, but sadly didn't have the time. Tarô is, I believe, working his way through the list of things I asked him to do. Have you heard any more from Hayashi of the Imperial Guards?

3. I am not sending letters out to anyone at all just now. If any soldiers from the old days or friends ask about me, just tell them that I have gone to the front somewhere in the south.

The first postscript shows that even before he had been there a month, Kuribayashi was already sending home the personal effects he had brought with him to the front.

He must have realized once he got to the island that he would never leave the place alive. Knowing that his possessions would not make it back if he died in battle, he decided to send them back as keepsakes for his family while he still could. It's also possible that after he took up his appointment he simply decided that anything beyond the bare minimum was superfluous. As he wrote in a letter, Iwo Jima was like a desert: "To put it in a nutshell, we're living in caves in a barren wasteland like Iizunahara in Shinshû or Sugadaira, so, depending on how you look at it, our life is hell."

It was the second postscript that surprised me and really got me interested.

Here was a commander in chief in charge of more than twenty thousand men and he was worrying about a draft in the kitchen in his final message.

Kuribayashi was fifty-two years old. Just prior to shipping out for the front, he had been granted the honor of an audience with the emperor, who had wished him well in his endeavor. How incredible that such a man should have chosen to list a piece of repair work in the kitchen of his home among his last, lingering regrets.

Iwo Jima was the only battle where the Americans suffered more casualties than the Japanese after America took the offensive in the Pacific War. It was an extraordinary feat for the defending side to inflict so much damage on their attackers and to force the U.S. Marine Corps to fight the harshest and bloodiest battle in its history.

On the American side, there were a total of 28,686 killed and wounded, while the equivalent figure for the Japanese was 21,152. When it comes to the number of dead, the Americans lost 6,821 men, and the Japanese 20,129. Here the Japanese figure is higher, but when the enormous gap in military strength is taken into account, the overall picture remains startling.

The Japanese army was being defeated everywhere else and it was Kuribayashi's staunch leadership that pulled together an ill-equipped bunch of randomly cobbled-together units and enabled them to put up such a heroic fight. The enemy officers had a high regard for Kuribayashi. Lieutenant General Holland M. Smith, the marine officer who was in command of the assault on Iwo Jima, had the following to say about Kuribayashi in his book *Coral and Brass:* "His ground organization was far superior to any I had seen in France in World War I and observers said it excelled German ground organization in World War II."

"My enemy he may be, but I respect him" goes the old Japanese saying. A heroic leader of men, Kuribayashi caused the Americans more pain than they were to experience anywhere else.

But this soldier who masterminded a battle that lives on in the history books was also a husband who worried about the draft in his kitchen back home. Kuribayashi's unconventional final message makes clear that he was a man who existed in both of these worlds.

You can see how unusual Kuribayashi's final message is by comparing it with those of other soldiers. Despite being private and personal documents addressed to their families, the letters and final messages of the majority of fighting men were terse and unemotional. They bottled up their deepest feelings and kept things brief, and if anything, it is their manly self-restraint that makes them moving.

In the afterword to his book *Senshi no Isho* (*Final Messages of Fighting Men*), Handô Kazutoshi provides an example. It is the final message that naval ensign Yoshida Mitsuru, who served on the batttleship *Ya-*

mato and survived its sinking, wrote to his parents: "Please throw away everything that belongs to me. My only concern is that you all enjoy good health and live a long time."

Handô Kazutoshi was curious about the deep love Yoshida had for his parents and the various anxieties that lay beneath the surface of his austere final message, and he quotes a passage from *Senkan Yamato no Saigo* (*The End of the Battleship* Yamato), an account that Yoshida wrote after the war in which he reveals what his real feelings at the time were:

> What can I do about my mother's grief? Is there any way that I, doomed thus to die before her, can console my mother in her sorrow? Mother shall be left behind to bear the burden of grief in my place, and I have no way of thanking her for my life, the gift of her motherly love.
> Stop. Pull yourself together now. I am a warrior going to war. For me, the battle is everything. I must not think of my mother, her head bent in grief.

Yoshida, however, did not mention the feelings that were tearing him apart in his final message. His message was short and formal—as was thought proper for a Japanese fighting man.

Handô's book also includes the final message of Fleet Admiral Yamamoto Isoroku. It was found in his desk after his death with the inscription "Disposing of my Possessions."

1. There is a danger of secrets leaking out, so please deliver all my books, documents, and letters to the place that Lieutenant General Horie, class group head, designates.

2. From the rest of my baggage (there is one piece in Kuresuikôsha), any presents which I received in wartime

can be handed over [two ideograms in the original are illegible at this point] to be disposed of.

The message is terse to the point of being cold and brusque. This, presumably, represents the values of the Imperial warrior carried to their extreme.

Set beside final messages like those of Yamamoto and Yoshida, Kuribayashi's is very everyday, very family-oriented—even slightly effeminate for a military man of that time. That, however, is precisely what drew me to him. I found myself wanting to learn more about this unusual commander.

I researched his family and discovered that Kuribayashi's son, Tarô, was alive and well and living in Akishima in Tokyo. It was the autumn of 2003 when I visited him in his house in a quiet residential area.

It was an old detached house. The living room was not big and it felt cozy. The sliding doors leading to the Japanese-style room next door were open, and above the carved lintel hung a photograph of Lieutenant General Kuribayashi in uniform.

Tarô was seventy-nine years old. Tall and lanky, he somehow managed to squeeze himself into an easy chair, but every time his old cat scratched on the door leading to the corridor, he would get to his feet and open it. There was nothing in his gentle, slow way of speaking or his benevolent, slightly drooping appearance to suggest that he was the son of a "military hero."

Tarô had been a student in Waseda University's Department of Science and Engineering when Kuribayashi left for Iwo Jima. His major was architecture, and after the war he had practiced as a First-class Architect. Kuribayashi did not send his son to military preparatory school—something high-ranking soldiers tended to do—nor did he recommend that Tarô take the entrance exam for the Military Academy. According to Tarô, his father never told him he should become a soldier.

On the table lay a thick binder that Tarô had gotten out for my visit.

"Go ahead," he urged me, and I had a look inside. Sheets of yellowing writing paper were neatly filed in order. These were the letters from Iwo Jima.

The paper was probably military issue. There was a space to write the date and the page number, and "Kuribayashi Tadamichi" was printed on the bottom left. The paper was yellowing with age, but the finely penciled characters were so dark that they looked as though they had been written only recently.

The characters were crammed in tightly, with three lines of text to every two printed columns, and, possibly in order to save paper, all the letters had writing on both sides of the page.

The sheer number of letters took me by surprise. In the roughly eight months Kuribayashi was in Iwo Jima before the Americans made their landing, he sent a total of forty-one letters home, if you include the letters to his children. And the letter in which he had expressed his regret at not dealing with the draft in the kitchen turned out not to be his last letter after all.

AS I READ KURIBAYASHI's letters in chronological order, I realized that they all started with an assurance of his safety.

"Skipping all the opening formalities, I am hale and hearty as ever, so there's no need to worry about me"; "I am robust and working away, so there's no need to worry about me"; "I am really very well, so there's no need to worry about me"; "I am still safe and sound, so there's no need to worry about me." Given the circumstances he was in, Kuribayashi clearly felt that his still being alive was the most important fact for him to get across to his family. The first sentence of every opening paragraph invariably concludes with the phrase: "There's no need to worry about me."

It seems that he continued to worry about the "draft in the kitchen." The following passage occurs in a letter he wrote to Yoshii on November 28, 1944, five months after the previously cited one:

You haven't mentioned it since then, but did you block the crack in the kitchen floor?

Everyone was always complaining about how cold the draft that blew up through the floor was, so I meant to do something about it. I ended up going to the front without having done anything, which is weighing on my mind. Why don't you get Tarô to fix it right away?

While you're waiting for him to get round to it, either double fold some old thin matting and spread that over the crack, or cut some roofing paper (there's a bit left over from the air-raid shelter in the storeroom) to the right size and put that down. I suspect the roofing paper will probably not last all that long.

"If you do get Tarô to do the job," continues the letter, "I think he ought to do it as in my diagram" and Kuribayashi has added illustrations to explain the best way to stop the draft. The two diagrams, one from above and one from the side, with red pencil marks to indicate the places where the nails should go, make clear just how concerned Kuribayashi was about his family back at home.

On September 4, 1944, he had written:

I am sure you gave Takako some pocket money. [Takako was evacuated to her mother's village in the country.]

Did you remember to give her envelopes, writing paper, and stamps so she can write to you? Not to mention toilet paper, toothpaste, and other everyday necessities. . . .

On November 17, 1944:

Since we're talking about baths, you really ought to heat one up about every five days or so. Since there are so few of you using it, you can reheat the same water two nights in a row.

This is what you should do if you do use the same water two days

*running. When you get out of the bath the first night, stick your arm
right down into the water and swirl it round in one direction so that
the water spins around like a top. Now throw the washbowl in. It will
spin round and round in the water then sink to the bottom, but as it
sinks it mysteriously picks up all the dirt and gunk. (Take the washbowl out of the water the morning after.) Give it a go.*

And on December 11, 1944:

*I really feel sorry for the way your hands get chapped and
cracked when winter comes around and the water's cold. Whenever
you've been using water, make sure to dry your hands thoroughly
then rub them until they get warm.*

It's impossible not to admire the way he repeatedly sends advice and
worries about their lives down to such minutiae. What's special about
Kuribayashi is that he doesn't just say nice things; he always provides
detailed advice on how to deal with problems. He seems to have spent a
great deal of time thinking about home, trying to imagine the kind of
inconveniences his family was having to put up with.

The letters give one the sense that, though far away, he still thought
like the head of the household who wants to make life that little bit easier for his family. It's also possible that the time he spent conjuring up a
vivid picture of everyday life in the home where he could no longer be
made life at the front that much more livable for him, too.

The American landing could have come at any time when Kuribayashi was writing these letters. The air raids were growing more intense by the day; his attempts to dig underground defenses for an
all-out war of resistance were progressing slowly, impeded by the geothermal heat and sulfur vapor released by the digging. And every day,
caked in dust and sweat, Kuribayashi was taking hands-on control and
inspecting the construction of the installations.

Iwo Jima does not have a single stream; when the Japanese troops dug wells, all they ended up with was saltwater with a high sulfur content. The twenty thousand plus soldiers, including Kuribayashi, had nothing to drink but the rainwater they could collect, and this water, of which there was barely enough to keep them alive, was polluted, and many of the Japanese soldiers fell sick with paratyphoid, diarrhea, and malnutrition.

It was a bleak island where the only reality was war. Maybe the fact that Kuribayashi could turn his thoughts to the kitchen back at home gave him the opportunity to anchor himself to a more normal, more human way of life.

I asked Tarô how his father had seemed before setting off for the front. "There was nothing special or different about him" was his initial answer. His father, he said, was just as relaxed and easygoing as ever.

But later on, as I was asking him about the layout of the house they had lived in back then, he said, as if it had suddenly come back to him: "That business of how my father was behaving before he went off to the front. Now that I think about it, he was busy making some shelves."

"Shelves?"

"Yes. Shelves for the kitchen and other parts of the house."

A lieutenant general of that time had a social position equivalent, or maybe even superior, to a member of the cabinet in our times, and this was the night before he was heading off to a battle where he ran every risk of being killed. Nonetheless, the thought of the inconveniences his family would face after he had gone inspired him to pick up a hammer and put up shelves.

In a sense, the Kuribayashi household was not unusual. No doubt fathers all over Japan were doing work around the house for their families as they waited to be dispatched to the front. It was their last opportunity to do any do-it-yourself repairs. But Kuribayashi was different in one important respect.

At the front, it is the judgment of the commanding officer and the orders he gives that decide if the soldiers in his charge live or die. When a soldier is ordered to charge, he has to do so even if he knows that certain death will be the result. Kuribayashi, as commander in chief of both the army and the navy forces, was the one who was going to be giving orders. It was Kuribayashi who would be ordering people to go out and die.

Kuribayashi was also well aware that his task as commander in chief was not to achieve victory.

It was Prime Minister Tôjô Hideki who appointed Kuribayashi to be overall commander in Iwo Jima, and he is reported to have urged him to "do something similar to what was done on Attu." Attu is a small island in the Aleutian archipelago where, in May 1943, a year before Kuribayashi was sent to Iwo Jima, the Japanese had fought desperately in an effort to prevent the American forces from wresting the island back. They had been slaughtered down to the last man—a fate they called *gyokusai,* or "honorable death."

The Imperial General Headquarters ordered Kuribayashi to defend Iwo Jima stubbornly, but his being dispatched to a remote and solitary island in the Pacific was no longer about being victorious or driving back the enemy. Japan no longer had the power to do that. After the country's defeat at the Battle of Midway, it became clearer by the day that Japan was destined to lose the war as the disparity in military strength grew ever wider. How long could the island hold out? That was the only thing that mattered.

Retreat was not permitted, even if the Japanese were conclusively defeated. "Do something similar to what was done on Attu" meant they had to endure to the bitter end and fight until they had all been killed.

What, then, were they fighting for? If victory was not even a possibility, what overarching goal could justify the deaths of his men as "worthwhile and meaningful"? Kuribayashi, who knew better than anyone the might of the United States and who had been consistently against the idea of attacking them, must have asked himself this same question.

The day after he had bustled about the house making shelves in his role as father and husband, he arrived on the island where a battle he was doomed to lose would be fought—a battle he was doomed to lose, on an island where more than twenty thousand men would go to their deaths on his orders.

CHAPTER TWO

22KM² OF WILDERNESS

—

Seen from the air, Iwo Jima looks like an ugly scab stuck onto the broad expanse of the ocean. It seems so flat and so thin that you think you could pick it off with your fingernails, and no matter the weather it is always a drab brown in color.

The island has an area of only twenty-two square kilometers—less than half of Tokyo's Setagaya Ward. It is hard to believe that a combined total of more than eighty thousand Japanese and American troops fought a historic battle over this tiny isolated island. Iwo Jima lies on about the same latitude as Okinawa, but it has no white-sand beaches, no gorgeous tropical flowers in bloom.

The island is somewhat long and narrow, and runs from northeast to southwest. Its shape is often compared to a rice scoop or spatula. Its highest point is the summit of Mount Suribachi on the southwestern tip, which stands 169 meters above sea level, while a plateau 100 meters above sea level extends over the northeast of the island.

This flatness was the primary factor in the destiny of Iwo Jima. The topography was perfect for building runways.

The other Ogasawara Islands were too mountainous for airfield construction. Chichi Jima had a base dating from prewar days and also an airfield, but the uneven topography made it difficult to expand the existing facility or build a new one.

By contrast, Iwo Jima already had two airfields, Chidori and Motoyama, when Kuribayashi arrived to take up his post in June 1944, and a third was under construction in the northeast of the island.

A mere speck of an island it may have been, but it had three airfields. Iwo Jima could serve as an "unsinkable aircraft carrier" out at sea. In the Pacific War, it was the battle in the air that determined the outcome, making Iwo Jima an asset that both the Japanese and the Americans needed and coveted.

The initial plan was to place the headquarters of the 109th Division, now under Kuribayashi's command, on Chichi Jima because Chichi Jima served as the center of the Ogasawara Islands for command and control, communications, and supplies. Chichi Jima was also much more livable than Iwo Jima, where lack of water and the scorching heat made farming of any kind impossible.

Kuribayashi, however, was convinced that the enemy would come to capture Iwo Jima because of its airfields. He also believed that "the commander should always be at the front line" and decided to establish his headquarters on the island. He then spent the nine-month period between assuming his post and death and defeat together with his men on the island, never leaving it even once.

A second key factor in Iwo Jima's fate was its position. It was situated 1,250 kilometers from Tokyo and 1,400 kilometers from Saipan. If you drew a straight line between the two places, the island was almost exactly halfway between the two. Iwo Jima would clearly be the ultimate foothold for the Americans, who were fighting their way up to the Japanese mainland one island at a time.

When Kuribayashi reached Iwo Jima, the Americans were just gearing up to take the Mariana Islands: Saipan, Guam, and Tinian. If they succeeded in capturing the Marianas, Iwo Jima would be next on their list, no matter what the cost.

The Americans planned to station the newly produced B-29 bomber, the "Superfortress," on Saipan. But they faced four serious problems before they could send these colossal bombers in air raids against the Japanese mainland.

First of all, any B-29s that took off from Saipan would have to make the 2,600-kilometer-long trip to Tokyo without any protection from fighters.

Second, since flying such a long distance would require large quantities of fuel, the planes would have to cut down on the payload of bombs they carried.

Third, the planes had nowhere to make emergency landings in the event of mechanical failure or damage from enemy fire.

Fourth, the radar station on Iwo Jima was able to detect incoming American bombers and give the mainland advance warning. There was also the further danger of Japanese fighter planes based on Iwo Jima intercepting the B-29s.

If the Americans could get their hands on Iwo Jima, all these problems would be solved in one stroke.

Of course, from the Japanese perspective, the fall of Iwo Jima would mean the loss of a key position for the defense of the mainland. Were the Americans to capture Iwo Jima, they would be free to carry out massive air raids on all the major cities in Japan, and the chaos of war would engulf ordinary citizens.

Furthermore, unlike either the Philippines or the Mariana Islands, Iwo Jima was actually a part of Metropolitan Tokyo, and as such was a part of Japan itself. Losing the island, no matter how small it was, would mark the first time in history that the Japanese homeland had been invaded. This had to be avoided at all cost.

The American forces launched their invasion of Saipan on June 15, about one week after Kuribayashi had reached Iwo Jima. In a letter Kuribayashi talked about experiencing three air raids in the month he took up his post; these air raids were not random events. The Americans wanted to facilitate their invasion of Saipan by suppressing activity on Iwo Jima's runways.

Once ashore, the American forces got the upper hand against the Japanese thanks to their overwhelming firepower. Then, on June 19, not that far from Saipan, the Japanese fleet and the American task force engaged each other just off the Mariana Islands in a major naval battle called the Mariana-oki Kaisen by the Japanese—the Battle of the Philippine Sea by the Americans.

The Japanese navy, although vastly inferior in strength, launched an all-out counteroffensive dubbed Operation A-gô. They sent in the biggest formation they were able to put together: 9 aircraft carriers and 5 battleships (including *Yamato* and *Musashi*), 11 heavy cruisers, 29 destroyers, and 450 carrier-based aircraft.

The American task force that the Japanese were up against consisted of 112 ships in total—7 heavy aircraft carriers, 8 light aircraft carriers, 7 battleships, 21 cruisers, and 69 destroyers—and an estimated 891 planes. The Americans had roughly twice as many ships and aircraft as the Japanese.

The Japanese were crushingly defeated in the Battle of the Philippine Sea. The *Yamato* and the *Musashi* may have been undamaged, but more than half of all the Japanese planes were lost. The Battle of Midway two years before had brought Japan's run of easy successes to a dramatic end and put the navy on the defensive. Ever since, the Japanese navy had rested its hopes for a reversal of its fortunes on its well-trained combined fleet. This battle effectively marked the demise of that force.

The Battle of the Philippine Sea gave the Americans air and sea supremacy in the mid-Pacific, including the Mariana Islands and the Ogasawara Islands. The fall of Saipan was now simply a matter of time.

The Imperial General Headquarters made the decision to "abandon Saipan" on June 25, while Japanese forces were still desperately resisting the invaders. They dispatched the units they had planned to send to Saipan to the Philippines, Taiwan, Nanpo Shotô, and Iwo Jima instead.

This is the historical background behind Kuribayashi writing a "final message" to his family so soon after arriving at his post. It was now certain that Iwo Jima would become the front line of the fight.

On July 1, the Ogasawara Army Corps was established in Iwo Jima under direct control of Imperial General Headquarters, and Kuribayashi was appointed corps chief. He was also division commander of the 109th Division, but army corps chief was the higher rank.

The 145th Infantry Regiment and the 26th Tank Regiment, both of which had been scheduled to go to Saipan, were diverted to Iwo Jima and placed under Kuribayashi's command. These were both elite regiments and played a key role in the defense of the island. Imperial General Headquarters had written Saipan off after the failure of Operation A-gô, but it was now getting serious about the defense of Iwo Jima.

Prime Minister Tôjô had bombastically described Saipan as "impregnable," but that did not keep him from abandoning it only ten days after the Americans had landed. The policy of Imperial General Headquarters toward Iwo Jima was to chop and change in similar fashion. They had decided that Iwo Jima would be lost even before the American invasion began.

THE FIRST THING KURIBAYASHI did after arriving at his post was to inspect every inch of the island so he could get a firm grip on the topography and the natural conditions.

He needed to know the island inside out in order to decide what kind of defensive positions to build, where to build them, and how to confront the Americans. Making the circuit of Iwo Jima on foot only takes half a day. So Kuribayashi walked. With him was his adjutant, First Lieutenant Fujita Masayoshi, who had accompanied him from Tokyo.

First Lieutenant Fujita had been Kuribayashi's adjutant since his appointment as commander of the Second Imperial Guards Home Division in Tokyo, and had volunteered to go with him to Iwo Jima. A family friend, Fujita knew Yoshii and the children. He was the scion of a wealthy family and engaged to be married, so his parents had no wish to see him go. But Fujita's affection and respect for Kuribayashi were such that he overrode their objections, wanting to be with him right up to the end. Kuribayashi had forbidden Sadaoka, a civilian employee of the military, to accompany him, telling him to "value his life more"; Fujita, however, was a military man, so he was happy to bring him along. Kuribayashi loved Fujita like his own son, but he must have seen him as a man, like himself, who had chosen the "way of the soldier" and for whom risking his life at the front lines was merely routine.

The first place Kuribayashi went was Mount Suribachi, the highest point on the island.

Suribachi was a dormant volcano with an enormous yawning crater. True to its name—*suribachi* means "mortar" in Japanese—it was mortar-shaped. The south side was a precipitous cliff that faced out to sea, while the northeastern slope went down to the plain of Chidoriga-hara. This flat stretch of land where Chidori Airfield stood was covered in volcanic ash and looked like a nightmarish desert.

Beaches ran along both sides of Chidorigahara. Looking down from Mount Suribachi, the south beach is on the right hand, and the west beach on the left. As the coastline in the northern and eastern parts of the islands had cliffs, reefs, and high surf, the Americans were going to have to land on one of these two beaches. Mount Suribachi, with its unbroken view over the beaches, would clearly be a major strategic point for both the attacking and the defending forces.

The Motoyama plateau in the northeast accounted for most of the island's area.

This region was rocky, with terraces and hillocks. The ground underfoot was tuff, a stone soft enough to dig with picks and shovels. Tuff could also be used for building blocks, so it looked likely to be helpful for constructing defensive positions.

The geothermal heat that reached up to 140 degrees Fahrenheit and the sulfur vapor that wafted up from within the earth were problems. Building fortifications was definitely not going to be easy, but the only way to hold the island as long as possible was to construct strong defensive positions before the American landing. Kuribayashi started to devise a strategy to repulse the Americans, whom he expected to come ashore with overwhelming firepower.

Kuribayashi also had to think about the needs of the men who had to live packed together on the island. It was his responsibility to maintain the discipline and health of his men as they toiled away, performing maneuvers and building defenses under the harshest conditions. What, then, was Iwo Jima like as a place to live? As he explained to his wife, Yoshii, on August 2, 1944:

> There are so many flies that they get into your eyes and your mouth. There are ants everywhere—like the pilgrims all moving en masse to Zenkôji Temple—and they come crawling up all over your body, lots of them at once. There are cockroaches, too—filthy, grotesque insects—all over the place. The only good news is that there aren't any poisonous insects or snakes.
>
> For food, there were a few wild papayas and bananas, but so many soldiers picked them that there are none left now. As it's a piping hot volcanic island, vegetables don't really grow here.

Flies were such an annoyance to the soldiers that almost all the accounts written by survivors mention them. It also seems that there were great numbers of cockroaches, which were still a rarity in Tokyo back then. Kuribayashi, who was fastidious and liked things to be neat and tidy, was obviously affected by the insects, as he mentions them countless times in his letters home.

The soldiers on Iwo Jima, including Kuribayashi, lived either in tents or in damp caves. When the air raids grew heavy, they would spread blankets on the floor of the dugouts and sleep there. There was, however, no way to thwart the attacks of the insects.

When Kuribayashi got to his post, there were over six thousand army and navy personnel on the island. With subsequent reinforcements, the final number swelled to over twenty thousand. The biggest problem they faced was how to get drinking water.

On his first tour of the island, Kuribayashi realized there was not a single stream in the place, nor were there any springs. As the island was made of sand and rock, rainwater would sink into the ground in only an hour or two. The only way to get a steady supply of drinking water was to construct cisterns to store it in. The original inhabitants of the island had relied on rainwater for their needs, but that was only feasible when the population was a little over a thousand people.

Prior to the landing, American intelligence analysts estimated the maximum number of Japanese troops on Iwo Jima at thirteen thousand men. With no drinking water available, they judged that anything more than that was out of the question. But their forecast was off the mark. The Japanese were forced to perform a miracle: sustaining twenty thousand men in an environment that was hopelessly deficient in water.

Kuribayashi was always acutely conscious of this problem, and he sternly prohibited the wasteful use of it.

He was especially strict toward the senior officers, who tended to get preferential treatment. On one of his tours around the island, the sight of a unit commander rubbing himself with a towel soaked in water from a cistern drove him into a rage. He reportedly told the officer that he "deserved to be executed by firing squad," before giving him an earnest lecture and the warning that "on this island, a drop of water is as precious as a drop of blood."

Naturally, Kuribayashi led by example and cut down on his own use of water. He explained to Yoshii on August 2, 1944:

Since there are no streams and no wells, we collect all the rain-
water, which we then use very sparingly. To wash my face (actually
I just wash my eyes), I put the tiniest drop of water into the basin—
about as much as we used for Marie's bowl. After that Fujita uses it
to wash, and we carefully keep whatever's left over and use it for
washing our hands in the toilet. That's the state of things for us—
but the men cannot even do that much.

Marie was the name of a German shepherd dog Kuribayashi had been
very fond of. The men were amazed that their commander in chief
could take care of his daily needs—cooking and drinking aside—with
only enough water for a single dog's bowl.

Kuribayashi always went on foot to inspect the island's defenses.
Since Kuribayashi was originally a cavalryman and a celebrated horse-
man to boot, some of his officers recommended that he make his rounds
on horseback. (There were three horses on Iwo Jima.) Kuribayashi
never once rode, on the grounds that riding a horse would only make it
thirsty.

Many of the soldiers recall Kuribayashi turning up at the different
units unarmed, with a cane, and wearing *jikatabi* (rubber-soled, split-
toed shoes). He always had a canteen hanging off his shoulder. At the
time, the water ration was one canteen per person per day. Kuribayashi
followed the same rule himself. Some units used their precious water
ration to boil tea in honor of the commander in chief's visit, but Kuribayashi would never accept it.

WATER WAS NOT the only aspect of life where he forbade any difference
in the treatment of the upper and lower ranks. On June 25, he sent out
a bulletin called "Important Points from the Division Chief" to all the
officers and men. It included the clause: "Officers must pay attention

to what the soldiers eat. It is forbidden to prepare food for the officers separately or to be indifferent to the provision of meals for the soldiers."

In short, Kuribayashi was saying that the officers must eat the same as their men.

The entirely rational thought that officers needed to have a proper grasp of the nutritional condition of the men under their command probably lay behind this policy that officers and men should share the same hardships regardless of rank.

Having once decided that he would eat only what his men ate, Kuribayashi followed through. When liaison officers came over from the mainland or from Chichi Jima, he would sometimes open tinned food and drink a little whiskey, but on normal days he gave orders that he be brought the same food as the ordinary soldiers.

This irregularity greatly perplexed his orderlies. When it came to the division commander, they believed that everything, even down to the number of plates, had to be different. Despite being ordered to bring Kuribayashi the same thing the soldiers were getting, the orderlies were baffled and didn't know what to do. Kuribayashi smiled at them. "All right, then," he said, "just lay out the plates as usual," and he ate his simple fare with an array of empty plates spread before him.

The navy had access to transport, so navy personnel were relatively well supplied. The army, by contrast, had poor-quality provisions and not enough of them. It was not just a matter of water; fresh vegetables were also in short supply, and they had to eat dried vegetables instead—Kuribayashi, of course, included.

He sometimes grumbled in his letters home, as in the letter to Yoshii on November 17, 1944: "I'm eating nothing but dried vegetables every day. They're so dry and so hard that they're driving me crazy. Seeing that I don't seem to be getting any thinner, maybe they have nutritional value after all." Plainly he had fulfilled his goal of learning about the nutritional state of his men through direct personal experience.

Kuribayashi encouraged each unit to cultivate their own vegetables in an effort to address the shortage. And once again, Kuribayashi was the kind of man who did not just issue an order, but led by example, as made clear in his letter of October 10, 1944:

> *I was thinking that we need to get fresh vegetables any way we can, so we've started to grow them by cultivating the waste ground. The results aren't that great. No sooner do you think you've got a shoot coming, than in come the crickets and cockroaches and gobble it up.*

Only a month after this griping letter (November 17, 1944), he reported happily: "Thanks to our hard work plowing up the ground and planting seeds all throughout the island, we now have a tiny crop which, amazingly, we're able to eat."

Kuribayashi's habit of leading by example like this appears to have impressed his men. Major Komoto Kumeji, the adjutant general of the 109th Division, survived because he had to fly out to Tokyo for a meeting just before the American forces landed and was unable to return in time. After the war he gave the following account of Kuribayashi's way of life on Iwo Jima in the book *Tôkon Iô-Tô* (*Fighting Spirit: Iwo Jima*), by Horie Yoshitaka:

> As a leader, Division Commander Kuribayashi was strict about military discipline and believed in punctuality and prompt execution. At the same time, there was a side of his personality that overflowed with warmth. He was always making inspection tours of the island, and had a perfect memory for topography and natural objects. He personally directed the organization and construction of the defenses, and while so doing he would slip the cigarettes that were a gracious gift from the Emperor into the pockets of the hardworking troops, sharing them out. He used to brush his teeth and wash his face with a single cup of water.
>
> Even the headquarters started growing vegetables, and they

offered these around for cooking. They grew sweet potatoes, which is an all-year-round plant. We often used to pick just about a centimeter from the tips of the shoots, put them in hot water, add soy sauce, and eat them.

In July 1944, Lieutenant Colonel Asaeda Shigeharu, army chief of staff from the Imperial General Headquarters, visited Iwo Jima for strategy discussions. He had heard that fresh vegetables and water were in short supply, so he filled large baskets with freshly picked cucumbers, eggplants, and tomatoes and loaded these on the plane at Kisazaru Airfield along with some seventy-two-liter barrels of well water. He got to Iwo Jima and handed the supplies over to the soldiers on duty, who received them as if they were sacred objects. Things soon became lively with cries of "Hey, everyone! Bring your cups! Fresh water from the mainland's here!"

It seems that Asaeda had prepared a separate consignment of vegetables for the commander in chief, and after the war he recounted his experience of delivering it directly to Kuribayashi.

I gave one basket of fresh vegetables to the division commander. With tears in his eyes, the general ordered his adjutant to use his knife to chop the vegetables up into small pieces and share them with as many men as possible below the rank of regimental commander. He did not take a single scrap for himself. On the contrary, he gathered up some papaya and made pickles, which he gave to the people around him. It was impressive; he was like a modern-day General Nogi.*

---

* From "Iô-Jima Kaisô no Ki" ("A Nostalgic Record of Iwo Jima") in *Ogasawara Heidan no Saigo* (*The End of the Ogasawara Army Corps*) by Ogasawara Senyûkai Hen. Nogi Maresuke (1849–1912) was a Japanese general who took part in the Sino-Japanese War and the Russo-Japanese War, in which he bore the loss of his two officer sons with stoic acceptance. He and his wife committed suicide on the eve of the funeral of the Emperor Meiji, and Nogi became a symbol of loyalty and self-sacrifice.

—

IN MANY OF HER LETTERS, Kuribayashi's wife expressed the wish to send him his whiskey ration and extra articles of food, or to give them to the liaison officers who shuttled between Tokyo and Iwo Jima to deliver. Kuribayashi, however, would always tell her "I'm in a more fortunate position than the soldiers, so have quite enough of everything," or "The airplanes have more important freight to carry, so please don't send me anything except letters."

When Kuribayashi received some confectionery as a gift from the emperor, he sent it on to his family without touching it. It is rather moving how he adds a small note to his wife: "To be consumed only at home." As a commander, Kuribayashi was stern and fair, but within his own family he was a completely ordinary father and husband.

MINING SULFUR AND MINERAL phosphates was the main industry on Iwo Jima. The climate and the soil quality were so poor that rice could not be cultivated, and the island's only agricultural products were sugarcane and a handful of medicinal plants.

Nonetheless, when Kuribayashi arrived on the island, there were around a thousand full-time residents, the majority of whom lived in a village in the center of the Motoyama plateau. They were simple people who, though poor, were accustomed to living a tranquil existence.

During the air raids in June, Kuribayashi allowed the islanders, who had no dugouts of their own, to use the military air-raid shelters. Seeing the women and children running around in aimless bewilderment and diving into the air-raid shelter with whatever they had on at the time, Kuribayashi decided that the inhabitants should be sent to the mainland as soon as possible. He also thought that they would get in the way, and that having soldiers and civilians rubbing shoulders on such a tiny island was not a good idea.

The "Important Points from the Division Chief" that Kuribayashi published on June 17 include the clause: "In emergencies, there is nothing problematic about giving short-term shelter to the local people in the army dugouts. They cannot be accommodated after the air-raid siren has sounded the all clear or in the nighttime."

The civilian population could be accommodated in military air-raid shelters to ensure their safety, but they had to be sent back to their homes immediately after the air-raid siren sounded the all clear, nor were any civilians allowed into the air-raid shelters at night. Kuribayashi also ordered that women should wear *monpe* pantaloons when air raids looked likely to occur. Perhaps he was trying to prevent any problems of public morals.

Kuribayashi was a puritan. No "comfort woman" station was erected on Iwo Jima, and one theory is that this was because of Kuribayashi's disapproval.

The repatriation of the island's residents started on July 3 and was completed by July 14. Men between the ages of sixteen and forty without dependents were conscripted, and the staff of the weather survey station was put to work for the navy, but otherwise everyone left the island. For a period of seven months prior to the American assault, Iwo Jima thus became an island only of men, with neither women nor children on it. It was uncomfortable and it was slightly cold-blooded, but it was best for the military to make their battle preparations with no civilians around. It was because Kuribayashi made this decision at an early stage that Iwo Jima was fought over without causing any civilian casualties.

The conflict was already turning into a total war, with no distinction between the military and civilian noncombatants. The Japanese citizenry was expected, as the "people of a nation at war" to sacrifice

everything for the successful prosecution of the war. But Kuribayashi
had a firm belief that soldiers like himself existed in order to make sure
that ordinary citizens could get on with life as normal.

In *Tôkon Iô-Tô* there is an anecdote related by Sakurai Naosaku,
a civilian resident of the island who was the director of the Iô-Jima
Sangyô Company. In the first few days after Kuribayashi arrived and
before a proper headquarters had been set up, he rented a room in Sakurai's house to use as his temporary command center.

> I often had meals together with Kuribayashi on the veranda,
> and admired and respected him for the way he took the lead on
> saving water. One of the chiefs of staff, who had a mustache, and
> Fujita, the adjutant, dined with us.
>
> When the news of the fall of Saipan was broadcast early
> in July, I asked him: "So, Your Honor, will you soon be lur-
> ing the enemy here to Iwo Jima to give them a good thrashing?"
> Kuribayashi, who was always cheerful, replied: "We just haven't
> the strength for that. I'm afraid we're going to cause you all
> a great deal of trouble, but with things the way they are,
> there's just nothing we can do." I was really surprised at his
> response.

Presumably, Sakurai had expected to hear—as anyone would from a
normal general—confident assertions about sending the enemy packing
with their tails between their legs, but Kuribayashi was just not like that.

Small though Iwo Jima might be, for the residents it was their
beloved home. As soon as the fighting started, their houses and their
workplaces would be smashed to smithereens. This was Kuribayashi's
apology to the inhabitants of the island for being powerless to protect
them, even though protecting civilians was what the military's job was
all about.

—

WHAT WERE KURIBAYASHI'S thoughts about the coming battle at this stage? The remarks by Musashino Kikuzô below are from *Tôkon Iô-Tô*. As captain of the engineering battalion, Musashino lived in the same quarters as Kuribayashi for some time after he had arrived on the island.

When he wasn't performing his public duties, he would chat and laugh just like any other fellow officer. He really was a gentle, rather bookish sort of general. He once said to me: "I was in America for about five years, and their peacetime industries are very advanced. They're organized so that if a war broke out they could switch over to producing munitions within a few hours of getting a telegram. The Japanese war planners never even bothered to think about an important issue like that. No matter how many times I repeated myself, they just didn't get it. However biased a view you have, our chance of winning this war is zero. But we have to fight as long as we have the strength left to do so; we have to fight down to the last drop of blood."

I have quoted extensively from the 1965 book *Tôkon Iô-Tô*. My copy was actually lent to me by Kuribayashi Naotaka, the present head of the Kuribayashi family, when I went to visit the house where Kuribayashi Tadamichi was born in Matsuhirochô, Nagano. The book had belonged to Naotaka's father, Sunao. (Sunao, who died in 1998, was the eldest son of Kuribayashi Tadamichi's elder brother, Yoshima.)

In the book, somebody had underlined in red the comment reported by Musashino, the captain of the engineer battalion ("I was in America for about five years, and . . ."), and there was a handwritten note in the margin that said: "Uncle Tadamichi often used to say this."

As a soldier, Kuribayashi knew a great deal about the United States.

During his first sojourn there, from 1928 to 1930, while still a captain in his late thirties, he conducted military research; then, from 1931 to 1933, he lived in Canada as military attaché.

While studying in America, Kuribayashi lived in major cities like Washington, D.C., and Boston, as well as Fort Bliss, the Texas base of the U.S. cavalry regiment, and Fort Riley, Kansas, home to an infantry division. He visited New York, San Francisco, and Los Angeles, and even drove himself across the whole continent. The sense he had of the military and industrial might of the United States was based on his own firsthand observations.

There is no evidence that the Japanese army leadership took advantage of Kuribayashi's knowledge and experience. Quite the opposite, in fact. There is even a theory that he was seen as pro-American and given the cold shoulder as a result. The conventional view may be that Kuribayashi was assigned to Iwo Jima because he was regarded as an able commander, but there is another interpretation in which his American-style rational thinking made him unpopular, and a deliberate choice was made to send him to a battle from which he was sure not to return alive.

Nishi Takeichi Danshaku, winner of an equestrian gold medal in the 1932 Los Angeles Olympics, was another prominent military man who met his end on Iwo Jima. A first lieutenant in the cavalry when he took part in the Olympics, he was a lieutenant colonel by the time of his assignment to Iwo Jima. Thanks to his performance at the Olympics, Baron Nishi ("baron" is the English equivalent of the Japanese title *danshaku*) had become something of a celebrity in American high society and had many friends in the United States. At the time, the rumor circulated that he, too, had been packed off to a battle zone where annihilation was a certainty because he was perceived to be pro-American.

Putting to one side the question of whether or not Kuribayashi was "pro-American," one thing is crystal clear. Despite knowing very well that the whole war was reckless and ill-advised, he was still determined to do his utmost to defend the island for as long as he could.

—

IT WAS ON JULY 7, 1944, exactly a month after Kuribayashi had arrived on Iwo Jima to take up his post, and, by happenstance, Kuribayashi's fifty-third birthday, that Saipan fell after sending out a "farewell telegram" that read: "We will meet an honorable death serving as a bulwark of the Pacific." But even at this early stage, Kuribayashi had already formed a firm idea of how to prepare for the American attack and how to fight them once they landed.

After much deliberation, he selected a method that was completely contrary to the traditions of the Japanese army. And it was because of Kuribayashi's choice of method—a choice that was derided as rash and that aroused universal opposition at the time—that the name Iwo Jima ended up being etched so deeply into the histories of both Japan and the United States.

CHAPTER THREE

THE STRATEGY

—

Sᴇᴠᴇɴ ʏᴇᴀʀs ᴀꜰᴛᴇʀ ᴛʜᴇ ᴅᴇꜰᴇᴀᴛ ᴀᴛ ɪᴡᴏ ᴊɪᴍᴀ, ɪɴ 1952, ᴀɴᴅô Tomiji, an employee in the Iwo Jima field office of the Takano Kensetsu construction company, made a stunning discovery. Deep within a cave in the interior of the island, among the scattered bones and personal effects of its defenders, he found an army notebook. In it was written the following list.

1. We shall defend this place with all our strength to the end.
2. We shall fling ourselves against the enemy tanks clutching explosives to destroy them.
3. We shall slaughter the enemy, dashing in among them to kill them.
4. Every one of our shots shall be on target and kill the enemy.
5. We shall not die until we have killed ten of the enemy.
6. We shall continue to harass the enemy with guerrilla tactics even if only one of us remains alive.

These six fervent statements constitute the "Courageous Battle Vows" that Kuribayashi composed and distributed to all his men. The vows are basically a collection of slogans outlining a soldier's proper state of mind in which to face battle.

The same vows were found in other notebooks discovered on the island. According to a field diary discovered after the war, the soldiers used to recite the vows together at morning assemblies and other occasions.

The text and Japanese ideograms in the vows I quote from differ slightly from the "Courageous Battle Vows" in the official history. This is probably because each unit received a mimeographed copy from which the soldiers copied the six clauses into their own notebooks.

Andô worked hard collecting the bones and possessions of the dead from Iwo Jima while it was still occupied by the United States. He later said in his memoirs that the soldiers probably "regarded the vows as an article of faith, and, even after their bodies had rotted, were still reluctant to let go of them."

Bill D. Ross, who took part in the invasion of Iwo Jima as a marine sergeant combat correspondent, comments in his book *Iwo Jima: Legacy of Valor* on how many of the Japanese soldiers had copies of the slogans: "Marines found copies in the first destroyed bunkers on the beaches, and they would find others in caves, tunnels, pillboxes and other bunkers—and on the bodies of the enemy dead—everywhere on the island."

Over the eight months leading up to the landing of the U.S. forces, the Japanese soldiers read the vows over and over to imprint them in their minds. Kuribayashi urged his men to fling themselves against the enemy tanks clutching bombs, to charge into the enemy lines and kill them, to work on their shooting skills and shoot the enemy dead. You must not die, he said, until you have killed ten people, and you must keep fighting even if all your brothers have been wiped out.

This was not an order or a directive. It was an oath.

Kuribayashi did not say "Every soldier must"; he used the expression "We shall." The soldiers, in other words, were not being forced to do anything: When they fought to the death, they did so of their own volition. By implanting determination and pride through the vows, Kuribayashi was trying to sustain the fighting spirit of his soldiers, who were already worn out by their defense-building duties.

Looking ahead, the more than twenty thousand Japanese soldiers on the island clearly did fight the battle in accordance with the "Courageous Battle Vows." Their method of fighting was ruthless—incredibly so—and it terrified the Americans.

Even when the organized fighting was over and there were no officers left to give orders, the surviving soldiers evolved into guerrillas hiding out in caves. The last two Japanese soldiers didn't actually surrender until January 6, 1949—three and a half years after the end of the war, and almost four years after the fall of Iwo Jima itself.

KURIBAYASHI WAS A COMMANDER who "overflowed with warmth"; he was a commander who refused to eat any of the precious fresh vegetables brought over from the mainland, preferring instead to distribute them among his men. Yet this same Kuribayashi created slogans that seem almost too gruesome for our modern-day sensibilities. At the same time, they do show how Kuribayashi saw his role, and what sort of battle he was planning to fight. He knew the battle for Iwo Jima would not allow anyone the luxury of "fighting bravely and perishing heroically."

A single reading of the "Courageous Battle Vows" makes one thing clear: "achieving victory" was not the aim; it was "not to be defeated" for as long as possible. That was the goal for which everyone was to shed their blood down to the very last drop. Not being defeated was what the battle of Iwo Jima was all about.

Kuribayashi chose guerrilla warfare as his method—hiding underground, waiting for the enemy, and then launching surprise attacks; staying alive by any means possible in order to kill just one more of the enemy. His men would need extraordinary reserves of mental strength to execute this strategy. The "Courageous Battle Vows" were designed to foster that mental strength and reinforce their determination.

The battle of Iwo Jima was distinguished by appalling suffering. One soldier who survived commented in his memoirs: "There is a saying that 'the way of the warrior is to die' and we so wanted it to be a battle based on that ethos." To die a heroic death may have been the proper thing for a samurai, but Kuribayashi would not allow either his men or himself to indulge in that kind of ritualistic behavior.

He strictly forbade so-called banzai charges, those all-out attacks on enemy lines that ended in the annihilation of the attackers, and his men faithfully obeyed his orders.

Bill D. Ross describes the way the Japanese soldiers fought on Iwo Jima in the following passage of his book.

> Each attack was organized—not the screaming bedlam of banzais of other invasions, but missions with a purpose. Kuribayashi's troops were adhering to his "courageous battle vows" to harass the Americans "until we are destroyed to the last man."

During the merciless battle, the thought of bringing it all to an end with one final charge rather than fighting on through wounds, hunger, and thirst was tempting. On Iwo Jima, after all, victory or survival were not options. It was even thought that indulging the men in their final hope and letting them go out in a blaze of glory was a way for the commander to show the "compassion of the Samurai." But Kuribayashi was resolute: on this island not a single soldier was to be allowed to die in vain.

This decision was not based on any sort of humanism, but on hardheaded calculation.

Kuribayashi knew that he and his men were going to die, but he had calculated how to extract the maximum benefit from his life and those of his soldiers. Their role was to save the lives of the civilians back on the mainland, and to save as many of them as possible.

In the letters Kuribayashi wrote to his family, he repeatedly emphasized that were Iwo Jima to fall to the enemy, Tokyo would be subjected to intense air raids. At this stage, the air raids on the mainland were still only targeting facilities and factories connected to the military, but Kuribayashi warned them that if Iwo Jima were captured after Saipan, where B-29s were already being stationed, the cities of Japan would all have large-scale air raids visited on them.

In a letter dated September 27, 1944, to his son, Tarô, and his eldest daughter, Yôko, he said:

> *Tokyo is not experiencing air raids now, but if the island that I am now defending ends up getting captured by the enemy, then it's sure to start being bombed around the clock. (Just as the place I'm now in started getting raids right after the capture of Saipan.)*
>
> *The enemy counterattack is becoming fiercer and fiercer recently. It's only a matter of time before they come and attack the place where I am. When that happens, if we can't hold out, the next stage will be air raids on Tokyo.*
>
> *The awfulness, damage, and chaos of air raids are inexpressible and beyond the imagination of people living peaceful lives in Tokyo.*

To his wife, Yoshii, on January 21, 1945:

> *There are now 140 or 150 B-29 planes based on Saipan. By around April, that number will be 240 or 250, and by year-end it's likely to rise to about 500 planes—meaning that there will be that many more air raids than now. On top of that, if the island I'm on gets captured, there'll be an increase of several hundred enemy planes, and the air raids on the homeland will be many times more*

savage than now. In the worst case, the enemy may land on the beaches of Chiba and Kanagawa prefectures and penetrate near to Tokyo.

It was the desire to delay the B-29 raids and the resulting civilian casualties for as long as he could that made Kuribayashi opt for a war of attrition, no matter what the cost.

He also seems to have hoped that the army command would proceed with negotiations to bring the war to an end while he kept the Americans pinned down and played for time.

Funazaka Hiroshi, a survivor of Angaur, another island where the Japanese forces were defeated, has written numerous nonfiction works about the battles of the Pacific islands. In *Iô-Jima Aa! Kuribayashi Heidan* (*Iwo Jima: Alas, Kuribayashi's Army Corps!*) he includes the following anecdote:

At the same time as making his defensive preparations stronger, Lieutenant General Kuribayashi had something else in mind. He had been in America from 1928, and Canada from 1931, for military study, and he understood their fearful industrial power. When Major General Sanada and Rear Admiral Nakazawa were leaving the island, he asked them to deliver a detailed report that he had written to the Imperial General Headquarters.

The report urged them to "urgently appraise the fighting power of the American forces, and the economic strength of the United States, and make efforts to conclude peace after the fall of Saipan."

Typically for staff officers of the time, they did nothing more than exchange looks of astonishment. Worried that Kuribayashi's report would sap the fighting spirit of the unit, they kept it to themselves and never breathed a word about it to anybody else even after getting back to the mainland.

Major General Sanada and Rear Admiral Nakazawa were the operations chiefs of the Army and Navy General Staffs, respectively, who flew over from Imperial General Headquarters in August 1944 to inspect Iwo Jima.

Naturally enough, this episode does not appear in the official history. But in the course of interviewing many different people about the incident, I was told that a soldier had seen Kuribayashi discreetly slipping a letter to Major General Sanada as he was leaving with the words, "This is what I really think." The soldier in question survived the battle but is now dead. He is said to have worked near Kuribayashi in the staff officer section at headquarters.

At this late stage, it is almost impossible to confirm whether this furtively handled report really existed or not. What is certain is that Kuribayashi did believe that "exacting the maximum bloodshed from the U.S. forces on Iwo Jima would work to Japan's advantage in negotiating an end to the war."

THE JAPANESE COMBINED fleet suffered an overwhelming defeat in the Battle of the Philippine Sea, and when Saipan fell on July 7, it was clear that Japan had no chance of winning the war. By August, when the operations chiefs came to Iwo Jima, Kuribayashi was convinced that Japan was doomed to defeat. Even some of the army leadership were starting to wonder how they could bring the war to an end.

A letter that Kuribayashi wrote to his wife on August 25, 1944, shows that he believed Japan's defeat was inevitable: "Henceforth our fearful destiny is to lose this war and there's no way of knowing what's going to happen. It is crucial that, woman though you are, you be strong—strong so you can live through it all."

And on October 19, 1944, he wrote:

I am past caring about myself and am ready, no matter what. But if we are defeated and the Americans invade via the Kantô Plain, Japan will fall into unimaginable chaos. What will happen to you, a mother with children? It's agony for me to think about it. Even if something awful like this happens, don't give up, be strong, be positive, and live through it all.

Normally, such a letter would not get through the censors, and it reached his family only because he was the commander in chief. Interestingly enough, the censor's mark stamped on Kuribayashi's letters from Iwo Jima reads "Fujita"—probably Kuribayashi's adjutant, First Lieutenant Fujita Masayoshi.

Either way, Kuribayashi knew that the day of Japan's defeat was not far off. We do not know if he sent a report to his superiors at Imperial General Headquarters urging an early end to the war, but we do know that it was for the civilians who would experience the "fearful destiny" of defeat that he devised his strategy of how to fight most effectively on Iwo Jima

"KURIBAYASHI WAS AWARE of American public opinion when he chose to wage a bloody war of attrition. He wanted to make the American people sick of the war by drawing out the battle and inflicting heavy casualties on the Americans." So James Bradley told me. Bradley is the author of the bestselling book *Flags of Our Fathers*, which was published in 2000 in the United States. James's father, John Bradley, went to Iwo Jima as a twenty-one-year-old medical corpsman and survived.

There is a picture widely seen as the most famous war photograph in the world. It shows six soldiers raising the Stars and Stripes on a mountaintop that is strewn with shrapnel. The man in the center of the group is James Bradley's father.

The place where this photograph—later awarded the Pulitzer Prize—was taken: Mount Suribachi in Iwo Jima.

The act of raising a flag on enemy territory signifies victory and conquest. The American people already knew every detail of the dreadful battle on Iwo Jima from news reports, but when they saw this photograph they became passionate about a victory earned through so much loss and sacrifice. The photograph became a kind of icon; it was turned into a postage stamp, and, after the war, an enormous bronze statue in Arlington National Cemetery.

After his father, a national hero, died, Bradley retraced his experiences. As a result, he knows everything there is to know about the battle of Iwo Jima. On reading his book, I was struck by the fact that, while few present-day Japanese are familiar with Iwo Jima, in America the story of the battle continues to be handed down from generation to generation, and Kuribayashi is greatly respected by military men in the United States. And thus it was that I went to visit Bradley in Rye, New York, in the fall of 2004.

Bradley sees Kuribayashi as "the man America respected the most, because he made them suffer the most," and during my visit he explained his favorite theory to me: that Kuribayashi had developed his strategy based on his awareness of the fickle tides of public opinion in the United States.

"Americans have always taken casualties very seriously. When the number of casualties is too high, public opinion will boil up and condemn an operation as a failure, even if we get the upper hand militarily. Kuribayashi had lived in America. He knew our national character. That's why he deliberately chose to fight in a way that would relentlessly drive up the number of casualties. I think he hoped American public opinion would shift toward wanting to bring the war with Japan to a rapid end."

American civilians were certainly following every detail of the progress of the battle on Iwo Jima with bated breath. The volume of news they received, and the speed at which they received it, were unimaginable by the standards of Japan at that time.

The *New York Times* ran no less than sixty articles on Iwo Jima between February (when the invasion started) and March. Articles sent from correspondents at the front would be churning out of the presses only twenty-four hours later. And while it took two days for photographs from Iwo Jima to get to the continental United States, their quantity and their quality were superior to any other battle in World War II.

The staff of the broadcast networks had also come out to the war front, and radio reporters made live commentaries from aboard the battleships anchored off the island, and from the beaches where the American forces had landed.

Amid this flood of information, the American people were horrified to learn that in the first four days after the landing, the battle on Iwo Jima had produced more casualties than five months of jungle fighting on Guadalcanal. Public opinion grew agitated, and there were letters and articles in the newspapers: "Please stop sending our finest youth to be murdered." "The commanding officer should be replaced."

Bradley maintains that Kuribayashi had foreseen this response, and that it was precisely for this reason that he opted not to fight and die in a blaze of glory, but to wage a battle of attrition designed to maximize the human toll on the American side.

Bradley's theory may be correct, but the war subsequently developed in a manner diametrically opposed to Kuribayashi's hopes. The United States did decide that it did not want any more of its young men to die, but the means it chose to bring the war to a speedy end was to drop the atomic bomb, which killed and maimed Japanese civilians in enormous numbers. This was something that neither Kuribayashi nor the twenty thousand soldiers who fought so unforgivingly could ever have predicted.

August 6, 1945; 5:55 a.m. A single B-29 bomber flew over Iwo Jima, which had already been in U.S. hands for several months. The plane was on its way to the Japanese mainland from Tinian in the Northern Mariana Islands.

"The pilot did not just go straight past, but flew a number of loops around the island," Bradley told me. "He was paying his respects to the almost seven thousand Americans who lost their lives there."

The name of the bomber was *Enola Gay*. Its destination: Hiroshima.

LET'S RETURN TO Iwo Jima before the American landing. Kuribayashi's strategy to hold the island for as long as possible can be distilled into two key elements.

1. To abandon the doctrine of defense at the water's edge, and instead place the main defensive positions in the interior away from the shoreline.
2. To build underground defensive positions, and make all the soldiers fight from these underground positions.

As Kuribayashi's plan ran contrary to the Japanese army's traditional strategy, he was going to need all his strength of will and powers of execution to bring it off.

The "doctrine of defense at the water's edge"—the doctrine abandoned by Kuribayashi as "ineffective"—involved crushing the enemy on the beaches, just as they were coming ashore. This was one of the Imperial Army's traditional tactics and had seventy years of history behind it.

An enemy who comes toward the land on boats invariably suffers a temporary loss of offensive strength at the point when it transfers from water to land. The "doctrine of defense at the water's edge" was all about making a concentrated attack precisely at that moment of opportunity.

Up to that point, this strategy had been fervently believed in, and it was certainly not without advantages.

First of all, the incoming landing craft made an easy target for the defenders on the shore, particularly as they all came in at the same time and were densely packed together. Meanwhile, landing craft had no significant firepower of their own, meaning the defenders had the advantage.

Second, it was possible to methodically pick off the enemy with sniper fire as they came ashore. Since the number of men who could land at any one time was limited, the defenders had the opportunity to eliminate them in sequence. There was no need to face a huge number of the enemy all at the same time.

Third, you could attack the enemy just after they had come ashore and before they were able to deploy any serious firepower. The defending side thus held a significant advantage right after the landing took place, and hitting the enemy hard during this window of opportunity was sure to yield dramatic results.

If you let an enemy with superior fighting power land unmolested, then your chance for victory was as good as lost. To repel an attacking force, the conventional wisdom maintained that you needed to build the key defenses at the water's edge, where the decisive battle would take place, and also position the bulk of your troops near the shoreline.

This doctrine may have worked well against a poorly equipped enemy on the Chinese front, but in the Pacific islands strategy of the Japanese—whether at Tarawa, Makin, or Saipan—it proved itself a complete and utter failure.

It failed because of American airpower. Before they started their landing operations, the Americans would launch massive aerial bombardments that would obliterate any defensive positions—and installations on the beach had no cover, meaning that they were dangerously easy to find.

Throughout the entire landing operation, intensive support would also be provided by naval barrage and air raids. This meant the overall offensive power of the American forces did not weaken significantly, even at the water's edge. By contrast, the Japanese forces on Iwo Jima could expect little, if any, support from either sea or air.

The traditional army doctrine of defense at the water's edge was worthless as long as the Americans enjoyed air and sea supremacy. Kuribayashi was the first to grasp this truth and he made the decision to abandon the old strategy at a very early stage.

The Japanese resistance would quickly collapse if he were to pour vast quantities of men, matériel, and weaponry into the defenses at the shore yet fail to inflict massive damage on the Americans.

Kuribayashi would not allow a spectacular battle at the water's edge that would culminate in defeat. He felt that his duty was to pin the American forces down on the island for as long as posssible while inflicting a maximum number of casualties.

Kuribayashi made up his mind to let the Americans land, and to get his men, hiding like moles in their underground defensive installations, to wage a thoroughgoing battle of resistance.

WHEN KURIBAYASHI ARRIVED on the island on June 8, defenses were already being built near the shore according to the standard water's-edge doctrine. By June 20, after inspecting every part of the island on foot and examining its topography and geology, Kuribayashi had made up his mind to jettison the traditional strategy and switch to a defense in depth. This, it should be noted, predated the fall of Saipan.

"Defense in depth" meant placing the main defenses at some distance back from the beach and giving up on the idea of making a general counterattack on the enemy immediately after they had landed. Moving the main defenses back from the shoreline meant bringing all the hard work of the soldiers who had been building installations at the water's edge to nothing, while the officers in charge of the construction efforts were predictably indignant. But Kuribayashi's resolve held firm.

Colonel Atsuchi Kanehiko was in charge of the "I Detachment," Iwo Jima's permanent garrison until the arrival of the 109th Division under Kuribayashi. Atsuchi issued orders for the construction of new defensive positions in the interior on June 23, after receiving Kuribayashi's new battle policy.

1 Detachment Order

1.   I Detachment shall temporarily halt the construction of defenses at the water's edge and will construct defenses in the interior.
2.   Every infantry battalion will construct defensive positions in the region shown on the attached map.
3.   The artillery battalions will construct positions near Mount Ôsaka and near Minami Buraku, and on the north side of Mount Suribachi in order to cover No. 1 Airfield.
4.   The 15th Fortifications Engineer Battalion will work with the infantry and artillery battalions to build the defenses.
5.   No. 1 Company of the 9th Independent Engineer Regiment will build the command center for the Division and the command center for the Brigade.
6.   The key parts of the defenses listed above must be finished by the end of June.
7.   I am in Motoyama Corps Headquarters.

Commander of I Detachment
Colonel Atsuchi Kanehiko

The order calls a halt to the building of defensive positions on the shoreline, and states that the interior defenses—or at least the framework for them—should be built quickly.

The construction of inland defenses started immediately upon the issuing of this order. As Kuribayashi had taken up his command only two weeks before, this was quick work.

Based on staff diaries and other sources discovered after the war's end, the official history describes Kuribayashi's new plan for the defense of Iwo Jima as follows:

> To create strong, honeycomb bases on Mount Suribachi and in the Motoyama area that can hold out for a long time and accommodate a powerful reserve force. If the enemy does attack, they shall be allowed to land. We shall attack them after they have reached the No. 1 Airfield, drive them back to the sea, and exterminate them.

"A honeycomb base" (*Fukkaku Jinchi* in Japanese) means a strong defensive position designed to allow long-term resistance even after the enemy has broken through the lines of defense.

Let me summarize Kuribayashi's idea simply:

- The aim is to hold out as long as possible, so key defensive installations will not be placed near the beach where the enemy lands, but inland on Mount Suribachi and in the Motoyama area. A reserve corps will be maintained in readiness for the enemy assault.
- When the enemy attacks, they will be allowed to land unmolested without any resistance at the water's edge. The counterattack will only get under way once the enemy has progressed as far as No. 1 Airfield, whereupon the enemy will be pushed back to the shore.

Mount Suribachi was a dormant volcano on the southwest end of the island; the Motoyama region was a plateau in the northeast. Kuribayashi decided to place his main defensive positions at these two points, both of which were away from the shoreline. Squeezed neatly between them was Chidorigahara, where the No. 1 Airfield (also called Chidori Airfield) was located.

Chidori Airfield was all of 800 meters from the beach where the Americans were expected to land. It seemed likely that the first thing the Americans would do after landing would be to try to capture this airfield, so Kuribayashi decided to make his first attack there.

If he put his key defenses on the beach and tried his damnedest to prevent the Americans from landing and the strategy failed, the island was sure to be overrun quickly. But if he could first lure the enemy into Chidori Airfield and launch an attack when they were caught between the inland defenses he had built in Suribachi and Motoyama, his forces could inflict damage on the enemy while also being able to withdraw into their positions afterward.

The ultimate goal was to wage a drawn-out battle of attrition. Avoid a showdown on the beach; launch one attack; withdraw; then start an intense, long-term resistance based on multiple lines of defensive positions. This was the plan of Kuribayashi the rationalist.

KURIBAYASHI'S IDEA MET with fierce resistance from the navy.

"It's outrageous! In full knowledge of the situation, he's planning to let the enemy land and then he's going to hand them a crucial airfield on a plate."

"Smashing the enemy on the beach is standard procedure in our island strategy."

Such were the opinions of the navy.

In mid-August, Colonel Urabe Kiyoshi, staff officer of the Third

Air Fleet, visited Iwo Jima together with Major General Sanada, operations chief of the Army General Staff, and Major General Nakazawa,
operations chief of the Navy General Staff. Urabe was emphatic about
what he wanted.

"It is imperative to retain the air base on Iwo Jima so it can continue
to serve as our unsinkable aircraft carrier. That is why we must annihilate the enemy before they even make it to the beach."

Urabe then advised them to build a large number of sturdy pillboxes
(small defensive installations made of concrete) on either side of Chidori Airfield.

At this stage, inland positions were already being built in Iwo Jima
in accordance with Kuribayashi's plan. Since the navy was providing
all the necessary weapons and material for this, Staff Officer Urabe
pressed the army to loan manpower to the navy for the construction of
shoreline defenses. The navy was insistent that "This is what central
command wants." Kuribayashi did not deviate from his policy of building the key defensive positions inland rather than at the water's edge.
After all, it was all very well for the navy to talk about "unsinkable aircraft carriers," but by August 10, the total number of functioning planes
on Iwo Jima was paltry: eleven Zero fighters, two shipboard attack
planes, and two night fighters.

In the end, Kuribayashi promised army cooperation for the building
of navy pillboxes at the shoreline. He thought the material the navy said
it would provide could come in handy for building the army's underground installations.

But the materials were not delivered according to the original
agreement, and both cement and dynamite were in very short supply
on Iwo Jima. Kuribayashi is thought to have negotiated terms whereby
half of the munitions and material supplied by the navy would go into
building pillboxes on the beach, while the rest would be for the use of
the army.

After the war, Major Horie Yoshitaka and Major Shirakata Fujie, who were army staff officers in the 109th Division, reminisced about Kuribayashi's approach.

"The commander in chief was still a firm believer in inland defensive positions. If the navy provided him with the materials to build strong pillboxes on the beach, he planned to offer them a proportion of the army's manpower and to use the materials he received in return for that in a more effective manner. He thought the defenses on the shoreline should be decoys to draw the fire of the enemy's naval guns" (from the official history).

Staff Officer Horie secured Kuribayashi's agreement on August 18. He immediately sent a telegram to the combined fleet commander in the navy section of the Imperial General Headquarters.

> . . . Based on lessons learned from many past battles, we believe that the best way to defend this island is by destroying the enemy landing force and, in particular, boats transporting tanks and heavy artillery, before they reach the shore.
>
> The army and navy here are of completely the same opinion with regard to this matter. In order that we can do this, please persuade the various departments at central command and make arrangements to procure the necessary weaponry and materials listed below and send them here as soon as you can.

The message includes the phrase "Based on lessons learned from many past battles," but the defenses of Tarawa, Makin, and Saipan—where the water's-edge doctrine had been applied—had ended in complete failure. The lesson that should have been learned from these battles was quite clear: "destroying the enemy landing force and, in particular, boats transporting tanks and heavy artillery, before they reach the shore" was not possible.

—

THE "NECESSARY WEAPONRY and materials" requested by Staff Officer Horie in his telegram were as follows:

1. Weapons
   [i] Seventy 25-mm machine guns (with 2,000 armor-piercing rounds, and 500 standard rounds)
   [ii] Fifty 250-kilogram rocket shells
2. Materials
   12,000 tons of cement; 750 tons of metal rods for reinforcing concrete equal to 282,650 cubic meters; 15 kilometers of No. 20 heat-reinforced steel wire; 60 tons of nails; 200 sheets of wrought iron; 20 small stone-crushers

Kuribayashi was true to his promise and helped the navy to build their defenses on the shoreline. All he received in return from navy central command in the way of weapons and material was three thousand tons of cement and seventy-five 25-mm machine guns.

An estimated twenty-six pillboxes were built along the shore near Chidori Airfield thanks to the cooperation of the army. They were obliterated in almost no time by the air raids and naval bombardments that preceded the American landing.

CHAPTER FOUR

RESOLVE

———

O N AUGUST 19, 1944, THE ARMY SECTION OF THE IMPERIAL GEN-
eral Headquarters, which had clung so rigidly to the doctrine of defense at the water's edge, finally changed its way of thinking and set
forth a new policy of inland defense.

The Imperial General Headquarters had been confident about the
defense of Saipan, which was designated a strategic point in the "national area to be defended at all costs." Once the Americans actually
started their landing operation, however, the defense garrison crumbled in no time. Saipan fell on July 7, followed by Tinian on August 3,
and Guam on August 11.

The Imperial General Headquarters recognized the gravity of the
situation and changed the philosophy it had followed up to that point—
one of "annihilating the enemy on the water's edge, or making a daring
attack on the enemy before he was able to establish a foothold on the islands in order to annihilate him"—and switched instead to inland defense.

This new policy was called "Key Points for Defense of the Islands,"
and it was transmitted not only to Iwo Jima, but also to the Palau region
(Peleliu and Angaur). It began with the following two provisions.

1.   The commanding officer of the defense garrison on an
      island must focus on holding out for a long time as we
      need to inflict the maximum damage on the enemy.

2. You are permitted to draw inland from the shore and choose positions that suit your needs. You may build small fortifications on the front lines of the main defensive positions in order to transform the whole island into a stronghold.

Provision One makes it clear that defense of the islands should focus on endurance and attrition.

Provision Two contains the most crucial element of the new policy. The key defensive positions can be selected as "suit[s] your needs" after "draw[ing] inland from the shore."

This amounted to jettisoning the doctrine of defense at the water's edge—the strategy that the military leadership had followed so persistently up to that point. With things as they were, even the Imperial General Headquarters was forced to acknowledge that it would be absurd to just keep on with the same old way of doing things.

But the policy switchover came too late.

Just like Iwo Jima, the Palau Islands were expecting the Americans to make a landing, but the building of shoreline defenses based on the traditional water's-edge doctrine was almost complete there. The American invasion was expected any minute, so they had neither the time nor the materials to switch to inland defense.

By contrast, the decision Kuribayashi had made meant that inland defensive installations were being built on Iwo Jima two months before Imperial General Headquarters announced its new policy. The defense policy that Kuribayashi had propounded immediately after arriving on Iwo Jima was essentially identical to the "Key Points for Defense of the Islands." It was based on a "war of attrition" and "abandoning the water's edge for inland defenses."

The case can be made that Kuribayashi's decision was the result of reaching the conclusion that anyone would reach after facing reality head-on and thinking things through rationally. But overthrowing precedent required conviction, self-confidence, and powers of execution.

In fact, the navy was not alone in its opposition to Kuribayashi's decision to abandon the strategy of defense at the water's edge. Senior army officers on the island also expressed very hostile opinions. Kuribayashi, however, was not afraid of going out on a limb, and he gave as good as he got.

The reason Imperial General Headquarters changed its policy was because it could no longer ignore the strength of internal opinion, which was convinced that the traditional ways of thinking were no good. Plenty of other people had also reached the conclusion that the doctrine of defense at the water's edge was no longer working.

Reaching a conclusion is one thing; creating and implementing a detailed plan rapidly regardless of any obstacles . . . that was something that only Kuribayashi could do. Yet at that point in time, Kuribayashi's plan ran contrary to the policy of Imperial General Headquarters.

Kuribayashi was always "precise in observation and bold in action." He examined things very carefully. Refusing to be governed by received opinion or precedent, he insisted on getting out there and checking things with his own eyes.

This attention to detail, which can also be seen in Kuribayashi's letters to his family, sometimes irked his subordinates. In *Tôkon Iô-Tô*, Staff Officer Horie Yoshitaka recounts an episode from the early days of defense construction.

I remember that First Lieutenant Musashino had made a report to the effect that constructing defenses on sandy ground was difficult from an engineering point of view. For around the next two hours, Lieutenant General Kuribayashi was going around in his car, getting out in different places, lying down, and pretending to shoot in my direction with his cane standing in for a rifle. He ordered me to do all sorts of things—"Get down on the ground!" "On your feet!" "Get down lower!" . . . Now I knew what the staff officers and adjutants meant when they said, "It's terrible. He's such a stickler for detail."

Staff Officer Horie also mentions that the detail-obsessed Kuribayashi never hesitated or compromised when it came to deciding on, and executing, strategy.

> I don't know where that steely force of character came from. Maybe it was something that ran in the Kuribayashi blood. He had no hesitation about saying exactly what he thought in front of other people, and once he'd had his say, he was high-handed and wouldn't listen to other people's opinions. . . . Mild-mannered people found it hard to deal with the division commander's strength of will. In the end, the chief of staff and the brigade commander were transferred, and an authority on infantry battles came in.

From the autumn of 1944, Kuribayashi started transferring officers who had different ideas about strategy, or whom he simply judged incompetent. The brigade commander, the chief of staff, the staff officer in charge of strategy, and two battalion commanders were transferred in a dramatic shake-up. Major General Senda Sadasue, an authority on infantry battles, was sent out, having been appointed after Kuribayashi asked Imperial General Headquarters to give him "the best infantry leader you've got." Senda was a first-class commander with plenty of battle experience.

Kuribayashi's aggressive and imperious attitude exasperated some of his officers. They criticized him for "going too far," or for "having too much confidence in his own abilities."

The people who worked with Kuribayashi felt a mixture of shock and hostility at the boldness with which he tore up the rule book. In their responses to an oral survey conducted after the war by the War Department of the National Institute of Defense Studies, officers who survived the battle evaluated Kuribayashi thusly: "An intellect attentive to the minutest detail; a clean-cut decision-maker. He was the kind of general who would rapidly implement the decisions he had made, but it was noted that officers below the rank of chief of staff seemed to have a hard time keeping up with him." "He made a clear distinction between 'public' and 'private,' and in his 'public' role, his style of leadership was merciless, relentless."

Perhaps it was Kuribayashi's detailed grasp of reality that made him so confident in his own judgment, and so decisive in execution. It was commonly thought that people in authority should look only at the big picture without fretting about the details, but the optimistic projections of the war leaders who expounded on the general situation while ignoring the realities were all wildly off the mark. Policies decided on without any reference to the facts of the situation on the ground just made soldiers at the front suffer and ultimately led to defeat.

The grimmer the reality, the more commanders have to face it directly. James Bradley regarded Kuribayashi as "one of the few Japanese commanders of the war who calmly faced reality and was consequently unable to take an optimistic point of view."

Kuribayashi verified things with his own eyes, and never allowed preconceptions or wishful thinking to cloud his judgment. His strategy was effective in battle precisely because it originated from such a starting point.

Abandoning defense at the water's edge was not the only reason why the Japanese forces on Iwo Jima managed to put up such a heroic fight. The fact of building all their defensive positions underground was also significant.

Iwo Jima was very flat. There was almost nowhere suitable for placing a military stronghold. Ordinary dugouts or foxholes were not likely to survive for long in the face of ferocious American air raids and naval barrages.

Kuribayashi therefore decided that the best solution was to construct all the defenses underground, linking them with tunnels so the defenders could move between them. His walks around the island had confirmed that there were many natural caves. It would be absurd not to make use of them.

Arms and ammunition, equipment, manpower—the Japanese were weaker than the enemy in all these areas. Their aim was to hold out for as long as possible, so it would be rash to go for a head-on confrontation. Kuribayashi felt that hiding in their underground positions and making sneak attacks when the enemy was least expecting them was the most effective option. With such tactics, the Japanese could keep on fighting even when down to their last man. It was guerrilla warfare.

Guerrilla warfare is a strategy for resistance. The goal is not victory, it's not to lose. Guerrilla warfare is the only option available when the side that is inferior in fighting strength wants to wage a war of attrition against an overwhelmingly strong opponent. The communist forces led by Mao Tse-tung and the Vietnam War are both examples of this.

The garrison on Peleliu, a small island in the Palau Islands, mounted a heroic resistance based on the same approach as Iwo Jima— building underground defenses and continuing to resist the enemy with guerrilla attacks even as troop numbers dwindled—and it caused the Americans great grief.

Colonel Nakagawa Kunio headed the garrison at Peleliu. Under his command, more than ten thousand soldiers mounted a stubborn defense that endured for more than two months. His men supposedly created as many as five hundred underground defensive positions.

Peleliu, like Iwo Jima, had natural caves. Colonel Nakagawa chose the method of combat that would exploit these to maximum advantage.

On Peleliu, again just like Iwo Jima, the key goal of the Japanese was to hold on to the airfield, even though they had almost no planes left.

The Americans launched their assault on Peleliu on September 15, 1944, with a view to securing a foothold for the invasion of the Philippines. The Japanese were finally defeated on November 25. Over this time, the Peleliu garrison received *gokashô*—words of praise from the emperor for their gallant and tenacious fighting—no less than ten times.

Peleliu was invaded before Iwo Jima, and the defense strategy implemented there had much in common with the strategy employed on Iwo Jima. Kuribayashi, however, did not develop his strategy based on lessons learned from the Battle of Peleliu. The garrison on Iwo Jima had been building underground defenses for some time in line with Kuribayashi's strategy when news of the heroic resistance of the Peleliu garrison reached them. The reason these two brilliant generals devised and implemented the same strategy at almost the same time was because they both had the correct apprehension of reality, both refused to be awed by precedent, and both judged things rationally.

Coming up with the plan to transform an entire island into a fortress by building underground defenses was one thing; actually doing it was another. The physical labor the soldiers had to perform was almost unbearably grueling. On Iwo Jima, in particular, constructing the defenses was to prove extremely difficult.

The positions were built to a depth of fifteen to twenty meters in order to withstand bombs and shells. The Motoyama area, where the major defensive positions were placed, was made out of tuff, a soft rock formed by the consolidation of volcanic ash, meaning it was relatively easy to dig. The problem was the geothermal heat, which went as high as 140 degrees Fahrenheit, and the sulfur vapor that spurted out in places.

Ishii Shûji, a photographer for the *Mainichi Shimbun* newspaper, who was conscripted and served as an orderly in the 109th Division,

2nd Mixed Brigade field hospital, recalled the job of excavating the defenses in *Iô-Tô ni Ikiru* (*Living on Iwo Jima*), the book he wrote after the war.

> We would take advantage of lulls in the air raids and naval gun barrages to dig in places where the ground looked hard. We were just bashing away with picks, so even if we spent the whole day on the job, we'd only manage a meter at most. If we used a stick of dynamite, we'd still take ages to do two meters.

In places where the geothermal heat was high, the soles of the soldiers' *jikatabi* (split-toed rubber-soled shoes) would melt, and the sulfur gas gave them headaches and made breathing difficult. Dressed only in loincloths, they would work in five- or ten-minute shifts.

> The reason we did ten-minute shifts was because the geothermal heat in the cave was high and we were working in darkness—so even that ten minutes was extremely unpleasant. Our hands were covered in blisters, our shoulders got stiff, and as we gasped and panted in the geothermal heat our throats would smart, but there was no drinking water to be had.

At the time, the daily ration of drinking water was fixed at one canteen per person. Some survivors' accounts say that it was "one canteen for two," or "one canteen for four," but even that precious water was frequently polluted, and many of the soldiers suffered from paratyphoid or diarrhea. In *Ogasawara Heidan no Saigo* (*Last Days of the Ogasawara Army Corps*), one of the survivors recalled: "We gave the water nicknames like 'devil water' and 'death water.' It came from a well we had dug near the coast, so it was salty—and worse than that, it was hot."

They had to depend on occasional cloudbursts, when they would catch the rain on tent sheets and pour it into drums and water tanks, where they would store it. Whenever it rained, all the soldiers, including Kuribayashi himself, would grab whatever vessel was close at hand—cups, cooking pots, and buckets—and rush outside. Rear Admiral Ichimaru Rinosuke, the highest-ranking navy officer on Iwo Jima, would chant the lines: "Rain is the water of life. Outsiders cannot know how we feel as we wait for a cloud on this island."

Ishii Shûji, who survived and returned to his job at the newspaper, went back to Iwo Jima seven years after the war. He wrote about his experience revisiting the Command Center ("Kuribayashi Cave").

> I shone my flashlight around the walls and the roof, and then onto the floor, at which point the light bounced back at me. I did a double take peering to see what was down there. It was a puddle of water. Since I knew there was no underground water, the only possibility I could think of was that the water had seeped in from the outside. Over the course of seven long years, the rainwater must have made a puddle in the depressions of the floor of the dark cave.
>
> If only the water had been here when we were digging the bunker, I thought. Unconsciously in the darkness I walked around the puddle so as not to sully it with my muddy shoes.

This anecdote makes clear just how much the soldiers suffered from the lack of water. Once the Americans had landed and the battle began, the island's chronic lack of water ended up costing some of the soldiers their lives.

FROM THE START OF 1945, the digging of the underground passageways known as *dôkutsushiki kôtsuro* (cave-style communication tunnels) began in earnest. Once these were completed, they would enable the soldiers to move from one installation to another without having to emerge aboveground.

The American assault was expected any minute, so the work was done in shifts around the clock. Unlike the caves, the underground passageways did not involve simply digging down: they had to be dug horizontally at a depth of between fifteen and twenty meters below the surface, which made the work that much harder. And there was more than just digging to the task: the men had to carry the excavated rock back along the narrow tunnels, then either carry it on their backs or put it in crates and pull it up to ground level.

All the time they were working, the soldiers suffered from headaches and nausea caused by the sulfur gas. They had gas masks, but they were an old design and wearing them made them sweat heavily and made breathing difficult, so most men preferred to do without.

The poison gas and the heat were particularly fierce in the tunnel linking Motoyama and Mount Suribachi, so the soldiers nicknamed it "the tunnel of death." This tunnel was still unfinished when the Americans landed, with the result that contact between the two bases was cut at an early stage. This is one reason why Mount Suribachi fell faster than Kuribayashi had projected.

Forced to spend every minute of the day and night either in training or in digging defenses, the soldiers grumbled: Why did they have to suffer like this if they were going to die anyway? Some officers advocated canceling the building of the underground defenses: "We came here to make war," they said, "not to dig holes." But Kuribayashi was convinced that underground installations were the island's only hope, and did not let up in the demands he put on his men.

Specialists in the construction of fortifications came out to the island to take charge and incorporate cunning techniques into the construction: tunnels would veer off at right angles halfway down their length to neutralize bomb blasts, while entrances and exits were built at different levels to improve ventilation.

"We were divided into two groups and dug toward one another from either end so that we broke through in the middle. When we did, the air suddenly started to circulate and the geothermal heat, which had made it so hard to breathe until then, suddenly cooled right down."

So said Ôkoshi Harunori, one of the navy ground staff responsible for maintaining the transport planes that came in from the mainland. He helped dig the defenses in the intervals between servicing planes and repairing the runway. "Digging holes" was a task that involved every man on the island.

> With a view to carrying out general maneuvers and fort building in a timely and rigorous fashion, all officers and men, without any exceptions, must focus on maneuvers and fort building. In particular, the bureaucratic tasks at headquarters and administration center must be significantly simplified so that commanding officers of all ranks can get out on site as much as possible and devote themselves to leading from the front.

The above is a notice that Kuribayashi issued—"Iwo Jima, Key Points for Defense and Training." In it, he orders all the officers and men, with no exceptions, to focus on "fort building," or the construction of defensive positions. He also emphasizes that using administrative tasks at the headquarters or in the administration section as a pretext to avoid going out into the field is unacceptable. He believed that the only way to maintain the fighting spirit and discipline of the soldiers was for their officers to "get out on site" with them.

Kuribayashi also issued another notice—"Important Points from the Division Chief":

> There is no need for units to stop working and salute when a superior officer comes around on tours of inspection. The area commander can provide a situation report. The soldiers super-

vising operations should not be compelled to salute but should continue supervising.

The order says that the soldiers should keep on working, rather than stopping and saluting, whenever a superior officer comes around on a tour of inspection. Kuribayashi may have believed that the salute was a key part of military discipline, but practical considerations were paramount, and he was never a slave to form.

PHOTOGRAPHS OF KURIBAYASHI at this time show him wearing a soldier's open-necked shirt and *jikatabi* and carrying a thin cane instead of a sword. He made his daily circuit of the defenses dressed like this. He was always unarmed, not even carrying a pistol.

His favorite cane had notches on it, and when he went to check the progress of the work on the defenses, he would use it to make various measurements. Sometimes he would crawl into the tunnels on his stomach to make sure there were no blind spots; sometimes he would measure the thickness of the sandbags and direct the men to "make it thicker here." He would also get deeply involved during training, demonstrating how things should be done, even helping individual soldiers with their shooting action.

In the oral survey conducted by the War Department of the National Institute of Defense Studies after the war, Major Fujiwara Tamaki, a battalion chief of the 17th Independent Mixed Regiment who returned to the mainland at the end of January 1945 before the American assault, recalled: "Once it was possible to live in the bunkers, Kuribayashi would sit down on the tuff stone like everybody else and get on with his work."

Survivors often mention in their accounts how Kuribayashi would talk to them directly or give them the cigarettes that were a gift from the emperor. There are also anecdotes in which soldiers were startled to discover that the person who suddenly turned up unarmed and wearing common *jikatabi* was none other than their commander in chief, or ended up being escorted to their unit by Kuribayashi after getting lost on their way around the island.

Ishii Shûji, who, as a newspaperman in Tokyo, had known Kuriba-yashi, wrote about his experience of meeting him again as a recruit on Iwo Jima in *Iô-Tô ni Ikiru.*

That day I was walking along in front of the adjutants' room pushing my bicycle, when a general holding a cane came up on my right. "Uh-oh," I thought, and immediately stood stiffly to attention and saluted. The general in question was unarmed and quite old. It turned out that this old man was our direct commander in chief, Lieutenant General Kuribayashi.

The lieutenant general walked past me and said "Keep up the good work." When I heard that "Keep up the good work," I thought "No, it can't be" and took a careful look at his face; it was then that I realized it was Lieutenant General Kuribayashi whom I had met often in the course of my work when he commanded the Second Imperial Guards Home Division. So it was that Kuribayashi! [omission]

When the lieutenant general heard my voice, he walked back two or three steps, and looked me in the face. "Ah, you work for that newspaper—Ish-, Ish- . . . Got it, it's Mister Ishii." And he smiled.

"Yes, I'm Ishii. I used to work at the *Mainichi Shimbun.*" On my side I was thrilled that he had not forgotten who I was, and I spoke this unnecessarily loudly.

"So, young Mister Ishii, is it? Funny place for us to meet, eh! When did you get here?—Oh, of course, of course, I suppose it was only about three months ago. When you've got time, drop in for a visit," he said and then slowly went on his way.

Tada Minoru, a graduate of the Naval Preparatory School and a survivor who was sent to Iwo Jima as a lieutenant, wrote about his memories of Kuribayashi in his book *Nanimo Kataranakatta Seishun* (*Youth That Could Not Have Its Say*).

> One day, out of the blue, there was an inspection of our emplacement by the commander in chief. Captain Wachi himself was driving the car. It was Lieutenant General Kuribayashi, commanding officer of the 109th Division, who had just taken up his post as leader of the Ogasawara Army Corps.
>
> "Southern coast machine-gun emplacement. Weapons and personnel all in order."
>
> As Tada made his report, Captain Wachi, who was standing nearby, added, "Tada is the emplacement commander."
>
> "This is a difficult place you've got here."
>
> Lieutenant General Kuribayashi took a good look at the gun emplacement and at the beach directly below.
>
> "You were at the naval school, Lieutenant Tada?"
>
> "Yes, sir. I was."
>
> "I'll be asking a lot from you. I'm depending on you to stand firm."
>
> As Lieutenant General Kuribayashi said this he moved on to the next gun emplacement. The expression in his eyes was kind and stern at the same time.

In the documentation on the American side, there is an account that notes with surprise that the majority of the Japanese who became prisoners of war had seen Kuribayashi face-to-face. On a front where more than twenty thousand soldiers were stationed, it was hard to conceive that the greater part of them should have met their commander in chief.

In a place where living conditions were as harsh as Iwo Jima, morale would quickly sink if there was insufficient contact between the officers and the men. Even if the ordinary soldiers never actually got to see his face, word getting around that the commander in chief—that lofty, superior being—was inspecting the defenses on a daily basis helped to boost their spirits.

It is estimated that the underground defenses were seventy percent complete when the American landing operation got under way in February 1945. Kuribayashi was no doubt frustrated that he was not vouchsafed a little more time and a greater quantity of materials, but the work proceeded surprisingly smoothly in light of all the difficulties involved.

"It's a miracle that the soldiers could stand the stress of spending eight whole months on an island with no alcohol, no entertainment, and not a single woman," James Bradley told me.

Major Fujiwara Tamaki revealed what he felt about his time on the island.

There was absolutely nothing on Iwo Jima and it was a dreary place. Even if we were given money there was nothing we could buy; there were only military personnel there; on a fine day you could more or less make out Kita Iwo Jima, but aside from that there was nothing but sea. After about six months, I thought I was going to go crazy.

The sense of isolation on Iwo Jima only increased the stress the soldiers had to put up with as they waited for the American assault, grinding away at their exhausting tasks, short of water and food. Nonetheless, the military discipline of the Iwo Jima garrison was maintained over the eight months that they worked day and night training and constructing defenses, while avoiding air raids and naval bombardments.

AS PROPOUNDED IN THE "courageous battle vows," Kuribayashi's strategy was to ask the soldiers to die for him after fighting an agonizing battle. In a sense, that battle actually started long before the American landing.

A commander in chief sends the soldiers he commands off to their deaths based upon his personal judgment. It is an almost intolerably heavy responsibility for anyone to bear. High-ranking military men who find themselves in this position always try to find a way to live with the burden.

There are some who see their own superior abilities as justification for sending soldiers to their deaths; other leaders, like Nogi Maresuke, cope by applying standards of superhuman stoicism to themselves; most common, perhaps, are those who seek support from religious belief.

Kuribayashi fits none of the above categories: he was a realist and a rationalist. Letters like this one, which he sent his wife, Yoshii, on January 28, 1945, show that he was not interested in leaning on religious belief.

> *It's probably due to the strength of the faith of your grandmother in Higano* [Higano, in Nagano Prefecture, was the hometown of Kuribayashi's wife] *that she managed to get through the air raid without being afraid by chanting "Dainichi Buddha."*
>
> *But bombs and incendiaries fall quite randomly anywhere and everywhere, so faith is no use at all. Her faith may help keep her spirits up and that's all well and good, but she should be very careful not to come to grief by neglecting the various mental and practical preparations that air raids demand.*

I know from our experience here that the people who get compla-
cent and aren't serious about taking shelter are the ones who end up
getting killed or wounded.

SO HOW DID KURIBAYASHI reconcile himself to his role?

Kuribayashi knew that he would have to force his soldiers to die a cruel death—and that was the reason he made up his mind to stay with them on Iwo Jima. He refused to exercise his command from Chichi Jima, which was safe and had water and food in abundance. Instead, he went to Iwo Jima and did not leave the island again until he died there.

The defense of the Ogasawara Islands, including Iwo Jima, had been in the hands of Major General Ôsuka Koto'o, the Ogasawara Region group commander, until Kuribayashi's arrival. Ôsuka had exercised his command from Chichi Jima, and he naturally assumed that Kuribayashi would do the same. Indeed, it was not until the battle had progressed to a certain point that even the Americans realized that the commander in chief was in direct control on an island that their preliminary air raids and naval bombardments had transformed into so much scorched ground.

According to Kuribayashi's son, Tarô, the family discovered that Kuribayashi was in Iwo Jima in the fall of 1944, when one of his subordinates, who was briefly in Tokyo for business, dropped into the house in Higashi Matsubara. Kuribayashi's wife would also have preferred him to be in Chichi, rather than Iwo Jima, and seems to have sent him a letter that said, "Adjutant Fujita's father says Chichi Jima is safer, too." Kuribayashi replied to her on November 2, 1945:

You tell me that Fujita's father said that Chichi Jima was likely
to be safer than Iwo Jima. I think he's right. But to protect Japan it's
much more important for me to be in Iwo Jima—and that's why I'm
here. I haven't the time to think about whether I'm safe.

———

KURIBAYASHI WALKED EVERY inch of the island, inspecting the construction of the defensive positions; he took the lead in efforts to save water; he even cultivated a vegetable patch. He refused any gifts of food and ate the same thing as his men three times a day. He imposed a regime on himself that made sure he experienced all the discomforts of the ordinary soldiers.

He made himself a part of the day-to-day life of his men, a comrade who shared their "life with no tomorrow." In the run-up to the American assault, Kuribayashi's resolve was to live the same life as his twenty thousand men.

CHAPTER FIVE

FAMILY

—

The evening sky is clear,
And the autumn wind blows.
The moon casts its shadows
As the bell-ring crickets chirp.

SHE STARTED SINGING THE SONG IN A THIN BUT BEAUTIFUL VOICE.
The sweat stood on her delicately powdered forehead.

"The young recruits used to sing this song as they walked back to
base after they'd finished digging the underground bunkers. Did you
know that there were sixteen-year-old soldiers on Iwo Jima?"

She pressed a lace-bordered white handkerchief to the corners of
her eyes and continued, her voice a little quieter now.

When you think of it,
It feels so far away:
The sky of home.
Ah, Father! Mother!
Are you both well?

"At sixteen, you're no more than a child. Just think how badly they
must have wanted to go home."

It was at the end of 2003 that I visited Shindô Takako in her house in Kawaguchi Saitama Prefecture. "Tako-chan," the little girl who had cried and made such a scene when Kuribayashi set out for Iwo Jima, was now sixty-nine years old.

The whole family agreed that she was "a chip off the old block," as bighearted and intelligent as her father.

Takako was calm as she talked to me about her memories of her father. Her voice faltered only once, when she started talking about her first visit to Iwo Jima after it had been returned to Japanese sovereignty.

"I think the place was called Mount Tamana. Anyway, when we got there, our guide, who was a survivor of the battle, told us that the young recruits often used to sing together as they marched through this area. 'Their voices were still the voices of children,' he said, 'and when Rear Admiral Ichimaru heard them singing he started to cry.' "

The song they used to sing was "The Sky of Home."

The youngsters always ended up singing this song even when they had started out singing war songs. It was a soft, sentimental song, and as it was deemed likely to undermine the fighting spirit, you stood every chance of getting a beating if an officer caught you singing it in the army of those days. But Rear Admiral Ichimaru, who happened to be passing by, motioned to an officer who was about to berate them to back off, then closed his eyes and listened.

One of those sunsets unique to the southern islands was splashed across the western sky, and the sound of the boys singing rose upward. Before the fighting started there were moments of beauty even on Iwo Jima—a place nicknamed "Black Death Island" by the battle-hardened marines, some of whom it drove to madness.

The young soldiers went to their deaths, their voices still the voices of children. Takako had been serene and composed when she spoke about the last days of her father and about the letters that begin "To Tako-chan," but she began to cry when she thought of those young boys. To me it seemed as though the grief of her father had traveled across a span of almost sixty years and was pouring forth through his daughter's tears.

FOR TAKAKO, HER FATHER was someone who was always kind and fun to be with, though he was often away from home. He was adroit—the sort of person who could turn his hand to anything—and would actively help with things around the house. He stood beside the maid when she was washing the plates and wiped them dry with a dishcloth.

The household had their maid when Kuribayashi was in command of the Second Imperial Guards Home Division. One day, when Sadaoka Nobuyoshi, the civilian employee in the military, visited Kuribayashi's house around dinnertime, he was astonished to see the maid seated at the table just like a regular member of the family. It was a highly unusual arrangement by the conventions of the time.

According to Takako, Kuribayashi liked to say: "Meals taste better if you all have a good time while you're eating. It's not good to sit around all stiff and silent as if you were at a wake." He often used to tell funny stories that made the whole family laugh.

In a letter from Iwo Jima dated October 10, 1944, he tells Tarô, his son, how he wants him to behave after he is dead: "When you're at home, always make pleasant conversation with your mother and your younger sisters; make the odd joke from time to time. It's important to make the whole house cheerful."

Kuribayashi had a sense of humor, something that was hardly typical of a military man of the time.

In his letters from Iwo Jima, he describes the stream of ants crawling relentlessly toward the soldiers' quarters as "pilgrims all moving en masse to the Zenkôji Temple." (Kuribayashi and his wife, Yoshii, were both from Nagano City, where Zenkôji Temple stands.) This particular figure of speech seems to have been a favorite, and appears in several of his letters.

Dumbfounded at the thunderous nightly snoring of his adjutant Fujita, whose bed was right beside his own, he writes, "When looking for a son-in-law, this is clearly the sort of thing one needs to check in advance—or else!" He continues, "Best not mention it to his [Adjutant Fujita's] father or anybody else, all right?" As his wife read the letter, she must have seen her husband's mischievous expression in her mind's eye.

Takako has fond memories of her father becoming "Mister Horsey" for her, and the fun she had riding around on his back.

Kuribayashi had originally been in the cavalry, and his skill as a rider was well-known. The story goes that, during his time at the Army Cavalry School, there was an unbroken horse called Tento. Tento had been universally written off as unrideable, but Kuribayashi, despite being thrown repeatedly, persisted until finally he was the only person able to ride him. This was the same Kuribayashi who would keep scuttling around on all fours until Takako told him that she had had enough and got down off his back. In fact, when I visited Takako's home, there were a couple of pictures of horses on the walls, one of which showed a military commander on horseback.

Kuribayashi was most worried about Takako among his three children. How would the loss of her father at so early an age affect her? He wrote her on September 20, 1944:

> *Every morning Granny is kind enough to pray to the gods on behalf of your Daddy. Thanks to Granny's prayers, Daddy has become cheerful tough. This war is a really big war now, so I really don't know whether I'll be able to make it home safely or not.*
>
> *If I can't make it back, I'll be most sorry for you, Tako-chan. But you make sure and do what Mommy tells you, and grow up fast to be a big, strong girl. If you do that, it will make Daddy feel a whole lot better, too.*

He mentioned Takako repeatedly in the letters he sent to his wife, as this example shows from a letter dated August 2, 1945:

> *Recently I had a dream. In it, I went back home where you and Tako-chan were thrilled to see me; but when I said, "I've only come back to make my will and I'll be going right back to the front," Takako was so miserable. In another one, I went on horseback to a temple. You and Takako had got there before me and were waiting for me. You were very surprised to see me—it was all so vivid in my dream.*

In a letter to Yoshii dated August 25, 1944, he wrote:

> *These days, I am enjoying every day I am alive, one day at a time. I have made up my mind to think of my life as something I have today, but will not have tomorrow. I want so badly for all of you to be able to live long and happy lives. I feel sorriest for Takako because she's the youngest.*

And on December 8, 1945: "I've been having lots of dreams lately, and you and Takako often appear in them. You both seem so real. It must be because you're the ones I'm most worried about."

"He was thinking about you right up to the end," I said to Takako. "Yes," she replied. "He was. And thanks to him I have had a happy life."

At the time the war ended, Takako had been evacuated to the country, but she soon returned to Tokyo with her mother. Her elder sister, Yôko, passed away immediately after the war due to typhoid fever.

Takako had good grades at school, and her mother, by working as an insurance saleswoman and a dormitory matron, was able to send her to university. Takako was studying French literature at Waseda University when she was selected as the "new face" of Daiei Studios. She told me that she applied not because she was keen to become an actress, but because she wanted to study traditional Japanese dancing and etiquette. Having lost their father, the Kuribayashis did not then have the resources to take extra courses outside school.

Takako fell in love with an assistant director at Daiei and retired after appearing only "once or twice in films where she was listed in 'The Rest of the Cast' section of the credits." She married him after graduating from university and was blessed with three children. She subsequently got a qualification as a nursery school teacher and worked as the head of a nursery that her father-in-law had set up.

"My mother worked very hard to send me to university. My parents-in-law also treated me very kindly, and I've lived my life without experiencing any real hardship. I'm sure that my father, who was so worried about my future, is very happy."

Then she thought for a while and added, "I think that my father was happy, too. He was able to live to over fifty in those difficult times and he rose to a high rank as a military man. Yes . . . I think he had a happy life. Really."

Without thinking I blurted out, "Do you mean even right up to the very end?" She nodded, and said "Yes" emphatically.

THERE WAS A REASON behind my asking so tactless a question: I couldn't help but think that Kuribayashi must have died feeling thwarted and frustrated. The more research I did, the more I realized how Iwo Jima had been abandoned even before the battle was begun.

With the defeat in the Battle of the Philippine Sea and the fall of Saipan, which meant that the "national area to be defended at all costs" had been breached, the Imperial General Headquarters formulated its *shôgosakusen*—meaning "strategy for victory"—on July 21, 1944:

We shall strengthen our defenses along a new line of defense running through the Philippines, Taiwan, Nansei Shotô, Ogasawara, the Mainland and the Kuril Islands. If the enemy attacks us anywhere in this area, the army and navy will immediately mobilize their forces and crush them.

Such was the new policy. If the new defense line were to be broken, then Japan would be finished. The so-called Victory Strategy was no more than a desperate last stand.

This strategy and the imperial mandate (the official order from the emperor, who was *daigensui,* or supreme commander) endorsing it were never transmitted to Iwo Jima. And this was despite the fact that Ogasawara was included in the "new defense line" that Imperial General Headquarters had decided to defend to the death. The Imperial General Headquarters had decided that the Philippines was a more pressing problem.

In August, Major General Sanada, chief of the Army General Staff, and Rear Admiral Tasuku Nakazawa, chief of the Naval General Staff, visited Iwo Jima. Four of Kuribayashi's requests on that occasion were recorded in the diary of Major General Sanada.

1:     At present we have only ten fighter planes (including one heavy fighter), and three midsize attack planes. When I left Tokyo, I was informed we would be provided with 48 fighters and 48 midsize attack planes. With current numbers, we are unable to conduct patrols.

4:     We are using only 12 to 13 twin machine guns. In total there are more than 160 25-mm twin machine guns available. The (infantry) battalions only have two light machine guns per platoon.

There were more than twenty thousand men on the island, but a paltry total of only thirteen fighters and midsize attack planes. Kuribayashi is also complaining that when it comes to weapons, each platoon has only two light machine guns. The ships that transported supplies to Iwo Jima at this time were often loaded with large quantities of green bamboo. If a ship was attacked and went down, the sailors could cling to it and swim; while, if the ship got through, soldiers could fashion the bamboo into spears to use in lieu of small arms on the battlefield.

Airplanes and weapons were not the only things in short supply.

5: I want thirty-five SB boats [1,000-ton second-class transport vessels] between here and Chichi Jima. I urgently want fishing boats and motorized sailing ships to be mobilized to make the trip between Chichi Jima and Iwo Jima.

[In Chichi Jima] there are enough provisions for a year and a half, but we only have enough for fifty days here. It is unacceptable for ships to transport things as far as Chichi Jima, and then just go back home. I want heavy and light machine guns to be airfreighted here. I was promised that 250 light machine guns and 160 heavy machine guns would be sent, but only one quarter of that number reached Chichi Jima. I also urgently need light trench mortars.

9: Since the start of June, we have had neither alcohol nor anything sweet. The navy have their PX [a shop where you can buy everyday goods, food, and drink] and they received an increase in the sake ration. It is not good for the difference in treatment to be so blatant on such a small island.

Clearly there were too few supply ships going between Chichi Jima and Iwo Jima, and the necessary provisions and weapons were just not making it out to Iwo Jima. There is something pitiful about the commander in chief having to beg for things to be sent to him even in fishing boats if need be. Similarly, "motorized sailing ships" were simply sailing vessels with a motor attached. Used for transporting freight along the coast, they hardly deserve to be called supply ships, particularly in wartime.

In this situation, Kuribayashi was desperately trying to figure out how to defend the island from an enemy who could attack at any time. In the end, only one quarter of the necessary materials that had been promised for the underground defenses actually arrived, while weapons and ammunition continued to remain in short supply.

Nonetheless, at this time the Imperial General Headquarters still appeared to take Iwo Jima seriously, regarding it as "a place requiring priority reinforcement as part of homeland defense." The strategy was to use concentrated airpower to annihilate the Americans when they attacked.

Things were in short supply on every front. The Imperial General Headquarters, which had overextended its battle lines, was busily devising plans and issuing orders, but was simply unable to dispatch the necessary materials to actually implement any of those plans. It was more than just a matter of a lack of supplies. Since Japan had lost naval supremacy, many of its supply ships were being sunk, so few made it through to their destinations.

As the tide of the war in the Pacific started to turn against the Japanese, the interest of the Imperial General Headquarters switched to the final battle on the homeland, and the defense of Iwo Jima was neglected.

The "Basic Principles of the Imperial Army and Imperial Navy Operations Plan," the first strategic plan of the war devised by the army and navy together, was drawn up on January 20, 1945. At this stage,

Iwo Jima was still defined as "an important territory that must be safe-guarded as the frontline of homeland defense."

That position changed on February 6 when, following on the heels of the "Basic Principles," the "Research into an Agreement on Army-Navy Cooperation on Air Strategy (Provisional Title)" was decided. This document declared that "Ultimately, Iwo Jima will inevitably fall into the hands of the enemy." This was the point when it was decided to abandon the place before the fighting had even started.

The reasons the Imperial General Headquarters gave were that since Iwo Jima was located "far away from the airforce bases on the Japanese homeland, exercising air power there is problematic"; and that "it has little value for the Americans as a base from which to invade the Japanese homeland." If they really believed that, why, one wonders, did they send twenty thousand men to the island? Their policies were so inconsistent that they seem to have been made up haphazardly as they went along.

In the end, the garrison on Iwo Jima met with defeat after holding out for thirty-six days. Few Japanese people know how heroically Kuri-bayashi and his men fought. The hell that they endured is now buried in history.

Takako is aware of this, but she still maintains that her father died happy.

"Why? Because no matter how awful things were, the soldiers all believed in my father and stuck with him to the end. Surely there's no greater happiness for someone in the position my father was in."

"Tako-chan"—now far older than her father when he died at the age of fifty-three—delivered this remark with a firm voice and a smile on her face.

I went to Takako's house three times to speak with her. The last time was a cold day in January 2004. She came down to the front gate to see me off and pushed some chocolate into my coat pocket, saying, "Have this on the bus on your way home."

It was six months later that I heard she had died.

KURIBAYASHI'S WIFE, YOSHII, had died the year before, in 2003. Her husband had written her: "Henceforth our fearful destiny is to lose this war. . . . It is crucial that, woman though you are, you be strong—strong so you can live through it all." And she lived on for fifty-eight years after the war, her long life finally coming to an end at the age of ninety-nine.

The Kuribayashis were married on December 8, 1923. Kuribayashi was thirty-two, his wife nineteen.

Kuribayashi had graduated from a middle school (under the old system), then went on to the Military Academy. After being made a second lieutenant, then a first lieutenant in the cavalry, he proceeded to the Army War College, an elite training institution where officers studied in order to command division-size or greater units.

Apparently senior officers approached Kuribayashi, who graduated from the Army War College second in his class, with offers of their daughters' hands in marriage. But Kuribayashi turned them all down to wed Yoshii, who came from the same region of Japan that he did.

Yoshii was the daughter of a landowner in Higano, near Kawanaka-jima, the site of a series of famous battles in the sixteenth century. Her maiden name was Kuribayashi, too, but this was merely coincidental, and they were not related. According to Kuribayashi Matsue, Yoshii's sister-in-law, the couple met at a *miai,* or "arranged meeting," that came about through the introduction of a dyer who was a frequent visitor to both households.

Kuribayashi seems to have doted on Yoshii, who was thirteen years his junior. After the war, Yoshii remembered her husband like this:

> He was very punctilious and exact; whatever he did, he liked to do it efficiently. But if I was working late in the kitchen, he would say: "Don't worry. Just leave things as they are and go off to bed." He was a very thoughtful person.*

With only one elder brother, Yoshii had few siblings for a family of the time. As a result, she was the apple of her parents' and her big brother's eyes. Her sister-in-law Matsue says, "She was brought up like a lady," and as an unmarried girl she was terribly shy. "When the draper came by and she had to choose a piece of something, she would be so embarrassed that she would run off into the back room and not come out." "Above all, Mother was a kind and gentle person," says Tarô, her son. "She was quite easygoing, and may have seemed a bit careless to my father, who was more highly strung."

Kuribayashi clearly worried a great deal about Yoshii, and the letters he sent from Iwo Jima overflow with expressions of concern for her. In earlier chapters I quoted from letters in which Kuribayashi was worrying about everything from drafts in the kitchen to her chapped skin and what to do about dirt in the bathtub, but there are also many passages in which he frets about her health, as can be seen from this letter, dated October 4, 1944:

> *Perhaps I'm just worrying too much, but recently I had a dream in which you looked terribly gaunt and your eyes were shining feverishly. Are you getting the massage lady to come? Make sure to take*

---

* From the series "Wives of the Famous Generals," *Shôsetsu Hôseki* magazine, November 1970.

a bath about twice a week to improve your circulation and avoid
hardening of the arteries.

And from this one, dated October 10, 1944: "Clearly, stuffing gunpowder into bags isn't an easy job. You must get stiff shoulders. I'm really sorry for you. It's important for you not to overdo it. Overdoing
things will be bad for your health."

Stuffing gunpowder bags is likely to have been a form of labor service, with each house having a quota to fill. Yoshii must have sent Kuribayashi a letter complaining about what awful work it was, and he is
writing back to her with extraordinary sweetness. After all, on his side
he had more than stiff shoulders to worry about, as with Iwo Jima subjected to round-the-clock air raids and naval barrages he was having to
sleep in an underground shelter.

As with this letter about stuffing bags with gunpowder, Kuribayashi
was always very careful to address all the points that his wife raised in
her letters. This from a letter dated August 31, 1944:

On the subject of using naphthalene to kill ants, these ants are
just not the kind of ants that you can get rid of that way. They're
all over everything—on the ground, on tree trunks, on the pillars
of the houses, on the walls of the houses. Unbearable. But at least
they go back to their nest at night, so there are far fewer of them
then.

And from September 20, 1944:

I read the clipping from Shufu no Tomo (The Housewife's
Friend) *magazine. Tragedies like that are happening everywhere.*
We're in a war, so be thick-skinned and just accept these things. If

you start worrying about everything that's happening, you'll just get depressed.

You might not expect a soldier at the front to have the time or the inclination to deal with questions about the suitability of naphthalene for ant extermination, or clippings from women's magazines, but Kuribayashi's replies dealt scrupulously with every point. For a wife to write to her husband, who happened to be a lieutenant general, about air raids and the course of the war would normally have been considered forward and impudent in this period.

Kuribayashi loved the childish sincerity and desire to be helpful that saw his wife trying to send naphthalene to the front. Clearly they had the sort of relationship where they could tell each other what they were really thinking. For his part, Kuribayashi shared honest opinions with her that he could not reveal to anyone else: "What a pity that I have to bring the curtain down on my life in a place like this because of the United States" (September 12, 1944); "If things were normal and this great war weren't on, we'd all—you, the children, and me—be having such a nice, happy life right now" (November 26, 1944). Reading their letters, you feel you are listening in on the couple having a chat.

From December 8, 1944:

You'll get cold sometimes when you're in the air-raid shelter, so you need to prepare a small foot warmer or a hot-water bottle. You'll need a blanket, too. And make sure you've got straw matting.

From December 11, 1944:

Please take good care of yourself. Make sure to wear a stomach band and a waistcloth so you don't get cold. Instead of underwear, I suggest you wear my camel hair shirt. I imagine there isn't much heat, so it's important to dress up warm.

From December 15, 1944:

Now, let's talk about clothes. In my previous letter, I recommended tie-up straw sandals, but what do you think about my old lace-up boots? The best thing is to try all sorts of things and see what works.

From December 22, 1944:

I mentioned my lace-up boots in my last letter, but they may be in really bad condition, so what about my army boots? You could probably wear them over your tabi *socks. . . . My army boots are in the box full of shoes that I tidied up. (It's in the second-floor guest room.)*

Holding them in my own hands, I read the forty-one letters that Kuribayashi sent home. Lofty terminology—words like "Emperor," "National Polity," "Sacred War," "Noble Cause"—was nowhere to be seen. Instead, there were footwarmers and hot-water bottles, stomach bands and camel hair undershirts, and boxes of shoes shut away in the guest room.

Kuribayashi thought hard about every detail of the domestic life of his family, and the same temperament was at work on Iwo Jima, where he carefully inspected the topography, made a daily tour of the defenses, and checked what and how much the soldiers were getting to eat.

There were stories that the commander in chief would often inspect the First Defense Line on his own. One day, when the members of the trench mortar company were all busily constructing their positions, Kuribayashi came to Mount Higashi by himself with his wooden cane.

The order was hastily given for them to fall in and stand at attention, but Kuribayashi told them to stay as they were. He asked how things were, went into the tin-roof barracks where they were in the middle of cooking, and carefully inspected the state of their supplies. Then he thanked them and went back to the headquarters. The bill of fare at the time was soft rice with powdered soy sauce, and clear soup with one or two bits of dried pumpkin in it.*

Kuribayashi planned a fight that was based not on empty ideals, but on deep knowledge of how people lived.

SO BOUNDLESS WAS the reverence that Fleet Admiral Yamamoto Isoroku had for the imperial family that he is supposed to have asked his subordinates about the weather in Tokyo every morning, even when on the front lines at Truk or Rabaul in the Pacific. He was terrified that the Imperial Palace might be damaged by air raids.

Kuribayashi was also anxious about air raids on Tokyo, and they form a persistent theme in his letters. In Kuribayashi's case, he was tormented by the image of his wife and children desperately trying to escape from a sea of fire. On September 12, 1944, he wrote to Yoshii:

> *As usual we're getting air raids every day. These days it's usually one or two planes in the night, and about twenty in the daytime. Our airstrips and our defense positions are damaged every time. As far as the eye can see, trees and plants are wiped out, and the ground is all turned over—a pitiable scene. People on the mainland cannot imagine what it's like. . . .*

* Murai Yasuhiko, "My Memories of Iwo Jima," *Kaigyô* magazine, July 1988.

*When I imagine what Tokyo would look like if it were bombed—
I see a burned-out desert with dead bodies lying everywhere—I'm
desperate to stop them carrying out air raids on Tokyo.*

And on December 8, 1944:

*In this war, there's nothing we can do about soldiers like me out
here on the front line dying. But I can't stand the idea that even you,
women and children on the mainland, have to feel that your lives are
in danger. No matter what, take refuge in the country and stay alive.*

Whenever there were air raids, he worried whether his family had
gotten through safely without him to take care of them as head of the
family. He seems to have been particularly concerned about Yoshii,
who was not that tough physically. On September 27, 1944, he wrote to
his son, Tarô, and his eldest daughter, Yôko, urging them to look after
their mother during air raids.

*You must understand that when there is an air raid the most im-
portant thing for you to do is to stop whatever you're doing, get together at the house, and do your utmost to protect your mother by
any and every means.*

*Even if the school has some rule about what you should do, you
need to think that our house could be burned down or you might die,
and you'll see there's no reason for you to blindly obey any school
rules. Just imagine that you go out to protect the school (though in
reality there's every chance that either you couldn't get there or else
you couldn't make it back), leaving your mother alone in the house.
How can she take care of herself when she's by herself? None of us
can guarantee that something awful mightn't happen to Mother if
she's all alone.*

Yoshii was adored by her husband; only once did she cross out any of the text of a letter he sent her. The passage occurs at the end of a letter dated January 21, 1945: seven lines of Kuribayashi's pencil-written text are blocked out with a black pen.

Tarô, the eldest child, deciphered the original text beneath the black ink and copied it at the time. Even now, with a little concentration, you can just about make out what it says.

The lines that Yoshii crossed out read as follows:

> *One more thing. In an earlier letter talking about cemeteries, I mentioned Gôtokuji Temple among others. That was because at the time it seemed likely we would settle in Tokyo, but now anywhere will do.*
>
> *There's every chance that my remains [will] be sent back to you, so we can postpone the whole cemetery issue. If I have a soul, it will stay near you and the children, so enshrining me in the house that you're living in will be fine. (And then there's always Yasukuni Shrine.)*
>
> *Last of all, take good care of yourself and live a long life. I am most grateful to you for being a devoted wife to me for so long.*

"I suppose the topic of his grave was just too painful for my mother," Tarô commented.

As mentioned earlier, Kuribayashi had said in previous letters things like: "Don't worry about what happens to me" (August 25, 1944), and "As I keep saying, screw up your courage so you can deal with whatever happens to me" (August 31, 1944). Maybe it was the detail with which he wrote to her that made Yoshii lose her calm.

Looking at the original letter, I noticed that there was another section, five lines earlier, where several characters at the beginning of a sentence had been crossed out. Holding the writing paper up to the light, I saw these words under the black ink: "As regards a final message, I have already written to you in detail about all the things you should do after my death, so, no matter what happens, do not be shocked or confused. I need you to be really strong."

This was the first time that Kuribayashi used the term "final message" in one of his letters. The phrase made his wife realize that the many letters he had sent her previously had been composed as "final messages"—written with the expectation of imminent death.

The Americans launched their assault on Iwo Jima twenty-nine days after he wrote that letter.

CHAPTER SIX

THE AMERICAN INVASION

—

Lieutenant general holland m. smith of the u.s. marines, the commander in charge of the assault on Iwo Jima, likened the defenses Kuribayashi had constructed on the island to a worm. This, ironically, was the highest compliment he ever paid anyone in the forty years he spent leading men in the front lines of combat. He wrote, in *Coral and Brass:*

> Like the worm which becomes stronger the more you cut it up, Iwo Jima thrived on our bombardment. The airfields were kept inactive by our attacks and some installations were destroyed, but the main body of defenses not only remained practically intact but strengthened markedly.

Smith may have been sixty-two years old and a diabetic, but he was handpicked for the job by President Franklin Roosevelt and sent off to the Pacific. A military man who had worked his way to the top, he was nicknamed "Howlin' Mad Smith."

Every force he led won.

They took large casualties on their way to victory, but Smith himself never shrank from danger. He hated military men who played politics and set little store by the lives of the men under their command,

and he had no hesitations about airing his grievances to Admiral Chester W. Nimitz, commander in chief of the Pacific Fleet.

During the invasion of Saipan, Smith had criticized the officer leading an army division placed under his overall command for "[lacking] aggressive spirit," and had the officer in question relieved of his command in the middle of the battle, which ignited an acrimonious dispute. He explained that he could not look on in silence while the lives of "my marines" (as he called them) were sacrificed by faint-hearted cowards. An insistence on sharing equally in the joys and sorrows of his men and a detestation of political maneuvering were characteristics that he and Kuribayashi shared.

Smith was well-known for his foul mouth, and while he calls Admiral Nimitz an opportunist in his memoirs, he does not stint in his praise for Kuribayashi.

> Of all our adversaries in the Pacific, Kuribayashi was the most redoubtable. Some Japanese island commanders were just names to us, and disappeared into the anonymity of enemy corpses left for burial parties. Kuribayashi's personality was written deep in the underground defenses he devised for Iwo Jima.

There is no one better qualified to judge a general than the enemy general he is fighting. They may never actually meet, but seeing how their counterparts fight in the extremes of battle gives them a sense not just of their abilities, but of their character and their humanity.

Lieutenant General Smith chose to compare the almost uncanny resilience of the underground defenses at Iwo Jima to a worm, and the comparison certainly encapsulates Kuribayashi's down-to-earth realism—his indifference to glory and to the conventional values of the Japanese warrior class—as well as the extraordinary strength of his will.

—

THE UNDERGROUND INSTALLATIONS showed their worth even before the battle started. They protected the soldiers from the massive
bombardments inflicted on the island as a softening-up before the
ground assault.

On December 8, 1944—almost three years to the day after the Japanese attack on Pearl Harbor—Iwo Jima was hit by the biggest combined aerial assault and naval bombardment since the start of the Pacific
War. For the Americans it was the anniversary of their humiliation.

Kuribayashi wrote a letter to his wife that same afternoon.

After touching on the usual everyday topics—"I told you before
that I don't need you to send me whiskey or anything else and I really
don't, so there's no need to worry about it"; and "I should be getting
paid an end-of-year bonus (2,650 yen, I think). It's a bore that no
matter how much I get given there's no way to spend it here." He
goes on:

> It's December 8 today. Just as I expected, we were attacked by
> large planes that came in thirteen waves from around 8:30 in the
> morning until about 1:00 in the afternoon. They were followed by a
> naval bombardment lasting one and a half hours, and I only just
> came out of the shelter now (3:00 p.m.).
>
> Bombs landed quite close to us, but luckily they didn't do any
> damage. The overall number of casualties is tiny.

On this single day, a combined total of 192 fighters and bombers
flew over Iwo Jima and dropped more than 800 tons of bombs. Three
heavy cruisers and six destroyers fired a naval barrage of 6,800 shells.
Aboveground, the Japanese lost 10 planes, but the underground installations were untouched, and casualties were almost nonexistent.

Up to that point the island had been bombarded in fits and starts, but from December 8 until the landing, the bombardment continued for seventy-four days without a single day's pause. Lieutenant General Smith and the rest of the American leadership were amazed that, despite a greater quantity and density of shells than at any other battleground in the Pacific War, the defensive positions continued to strengthen and increase in number over that period.

The Japanese soldiers would all dive underground when air raids and naval bombardments started, but when they were over, they would come back aboveground and resume their work. The intense bombardment had destroyed every single tree and blade of grass, but their underground world was unharmed.

According to the official history of the U.S. Marine Corps, a total of 6,800 tons of bombs were dropped on the island over the seventy-four-day period. In the five naval bombardments conducted in December and January, 203 16-inch shells, 6,472 8-inch shells, and 15,251 5-inch shells were fired. As far as the Americans were concerned, so intense was the bombardment that they wouldn't have been surprised if the island had simply ceased to exist. But the aerial photographs taken by reconnaissance planes told a different story: the 450 defense positions that had been in place when the bombardment started had increased to 750 just before the landings.

After the war, in his book *The Great Sea War,* Nimitz said:

> The Seventh Air Force B-24 squadron based in the Mariana Islands carried out continuous air raids for 74 days in preparation for the coming assault. These air raids only served to make the Japanese even more industrious in their efforts to complete their underground defenses. . . .
>
> The Marine commanders were well-known for their toughness and experience but they were flabbergasted when they saw the meticulous preparations of Kuribayashi's garrison in the aerial photographs.

Despite their lack of materials and drinking water, the Japanese soldiers on Iwo Jima had built a defense network strong enough to make the frontline commanders of the U.S. forces anxious.

The Americans nonetheless believed that five days would be enough to conquer the island.

On February 16, three days before the invasion, a press conference for seventy war correspondents was held on the command ship USS *Eldorado*. Marine Brigadier General William W. Rogers predicted that the Japanese army would put up a strong initial defense at the beach in an effort to keep the Americans from landing. He also said that the Japanese were sure to make a coordinated nighttime counterattack—a banzai charge ending in certain death—some time in the first night after the landing. The Japanese that the marines had fought so far in the Pacific had all followed that pattern up until now.

The Americans expected to take high casualties on the beach, but thought that if they could stick it out, everything would go their way.

The Americans were wrong.

From February 16 to February 18, the American forces pummeled Iwo Jima with naval guns and with planes, in preparation for the landing. After the war, Takahashi Toshiharu, a survivor who served as corporal in the First Mixed Brigade of Engineers, wrote a faithful account of his experiences on Iwo Jima based on his diary and notes. He wanted to forget what had happened to him on the island, but he also felt that it would be wrong to just consign it to oblivion. Of the 278 people in his unit, only 13 survived.

After Takahashi died in 1986, the notebook in which he had written his account was left in the hands of his family. It includes a description of the awesome three-day naval bombardment.

The guns that were trained on the island all spurted fire at the same time. On the island there was a huge earthquake.

There were pillars of fire that looked as if they would touch the sky. Black smoke covered the island, and shrapnel was flying all over the place with a shrieking sound. Trees with trunks one meter across were blown out of the ground, roots uppermost. The sound was deafening, as terrible as a couple of hundred thunderclaps coming down at once.

Even in a cave thirty meters underground, my body was jerked up off the ground. It was hell on earth.

The naval barrage was followed by a truly apocalyptic air raid. The explosions were so fierce that a quarter of the summit of Mount Suribachi was blown off.

Next, large planes—many tens of them—came all together. They made a deep rumbling sound as they came. They were silver. Once over the island they dropped one-ton bombs—terrifying things. The sound they made as they fell, one after another, was terrifying. A timid man would go insane.

They made a whistling sound as they fell. Then the earth shook. There were explosions. Rocks, earth, and sand all flew up into the air. Then they fell back down. They made craters ten meters wide and five meters deep in the earth.

No one could survive in these conditions. Any Japanese soldiers, like the runners who went outside, were all killed. The only option was to take advantage of the night and go out then.

With the advent of night, the Japanese came up to the surface and repaired their defenses. When the American ships fired off flares, they would again take refuge in their underground shelters, only to crawl out when darkness returned.

After three days in which the Japanese had endured a bombardment

1943. At the barracks of the South China Expeditionary Force in Canton, China. Kuribayashi sits (front center) holding a German shepherd. Sadaoka Nobuyoshi, an army civilian employee, who tried unsuccessfully to follow Kuribayashi to Iwo Jima, is standing behind him (third from right).

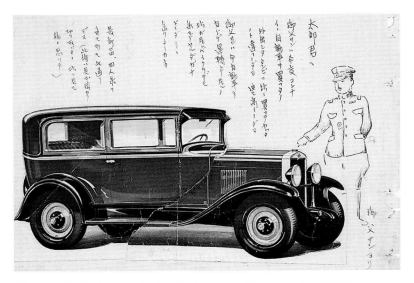

"Dear Tarô, I've just bought this fabulous car… if you were here I'd drive you around all you want. How about it? Fancy a ride?" Kuribayashi actually cut the illustration of the car from a catalogue and stuck it on to the letter.

Kuribayashi leaving his lodgings in Buffalo, NY, for Washington D.C.

昭和 19 年 11 月 17 日

たこちゃん！　元気ですか？　お父さんは元気です

ゆうべ寝て直ぐに明け方そう雨空襲警報が鳴りましたが

お父さんは面白いゆめを見ました

それはたこちゃんがおふろから上ってめそめそ

泣いておられたり

お父さん前にどうして泣くのおふわがあつかりがね。と

時ねむておるせお母さんが笑いふき出してお肌を出して飲ませ二人して寝ようにしておられました

ほしいからでせう。と言ふて

がりましたが其の時たこちゃんはのっぺをふくらしてスパくと飲んでもうこれと笑うにしておられました

おちち、を飲んでとてもこれと笑うにしておれました

が出て来てたこちゃんはこんなに大きくなってオッパイ飲むとはあき

れた

と言ひながらたこちゃんのほっぺたつきました

それだけですが、お父さん身みんなの面がはっきり見えた夢で面白いゆめでせう　どうぞ内地も今にあるかも知れ

會ったも全く久じでした

ませんが、たこちゃんのおる田舎はたいがい安心ですね内地はもう寒いでせう

こちらは空龍家はとても多いです

 たこちゃん！　信州の寒さは東京とは比べもの

寒いでせう　たこちゃん！

栗　林　忠　道

A letter dated November 17, 1944, that Kuribayashi wrote to Takako, his younger daughter, from Iwo Jima. Takako had been evacuated to Shinshū at the time. It talks about how he had had a dream of being together with the family.

Taken in August 1943, this is the only surviving group photograph of the family, showing, among others, Kuribayashi's wife, Yoshii (back row, far left); his younger daughter Takako (seated, third from left in back row); and his older daughter Yōko (front row, extreme left).

No.

お父さんも嬉しく思います
手紙の字は次の五つだけ間違っておりました
鬼蓄（鬼畜）、
撃滅（撃滅）　空龍板（空龍板）身体（身体）
次にお父さんの方も朝晩は少し寒くなりましたがまだ
夏服で居ります、草や木も青々としておるし蠅も

Like any good father, Kuribayashi corrects the Japanese characters that Takato had gotten wrong in one of the letters she sent him.

A letter dated November 28, 1944, with diagrams on how to stop the draft in the kitchen

From a letter dated June 25, 1944, the note outside the printed margin line reads: "Do not let anyone else see this letter under any circumstances. Do not talk about its contents."

A letter dated December 23, 1944, from Kuribayashi to Takako, talking about the four chicks he was rearing

A strategy meeting on Iwo Jima (top), and surrounded by the guards on duty (bottom). Commander in Chief Kuribayashi is in the center in both pictures. (Photographs by Shishikura Tsunetaka, Asahi Shimbunsha)

February 23, 1945, The Stars and Stripes being raised on Mount
Suribachi on Iwo Jima (top), and American troops moving forward
using a flamethrower to burn out underground bunkers (bottom).
(Photographs courtesy of Kingendai Photo Library)

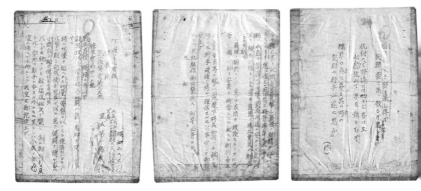

The farewell telegram sent to Imperial General Headquarters on March 16, 1945. Kuribayashi's death poem appears below.

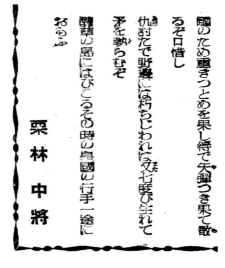

From the front page of the Yomiuri Hôchi *newspaper of March 22, 1945. All three stanzas of Kuribayashi's death poem have been printed, but the end of the first line has been changed to "mortified, we fall." (With permission from Yomiuri Shimbunsha)*

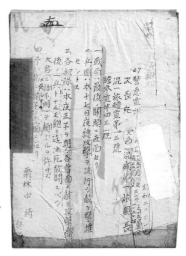

The telegram of early morning March 17 containing the rousing address to all the officers and men on Iwo Jima. The last line reads: "I will always be at your head."

fierce enough to shake the whole island, the day finally arrived: D-day, the day the invasion started.

3:00 a.m., February 19: The beating of the wake-up gong rouses the marines. Breakfast is steak and eggs, the traditional D-Day menu.

6:30 a.m.: The order is given for the landing force to land. The first of the landing craft is lowered into the sea.

6:40 a.m.: The final prelanding naval bombardment begins. Eight battleships, nineteen cruisers, and forty-four destroyers start firing their guns at the same time.

8:05 a.m.: Fighter planes take off from the carriers. A total of seventy-two planes take part in the attack; the navy fighters are Corsairs and Hellcats, the bombers are Dauntless dive bombers. Once they're back, the forty-eight planes of the marine squadron go up into the air for their turn.

8:25 a.m.: The naval barrage resumes. The scale of this day's naval bombardment surpasses the Normandy landings to become the biggest in the whole of World War II.

Such was the unbridled ferocity of the bombardment that clouds of dust and debris shot up eight meters in the air. In *Iwo Jima: Legacy of Valor*, Bill D. Ross, a former marine sergeant combat correspondent attached to the Third Marine Division, described the reactions of the marines who were looking at the island from the sea.

> Men on the jammed decks of transports, others in Higgins boats or in amtracs disgorged from LSTs, watched and wondered how any Japanese could survive.

In a similar vein, James Bradley, who interviewed many marine veterans for his book, has the following episode in *Flags of Our Fathers:*

> In these final moments, eighteen-year-old Jim Buchanan of Portland, Oregon, could still view the bombing as a beautiful

tableau, like in a movie; the island nearly invisible beneath clouds of gray, yellow, and white dust from all the rockets and bombs. He turned to his buddy, a kid named Scotty, and asked hopefully: "Do you think there will be any Japanese left for us?"

Was it possible that there were any living, breathing people left on the island, which now looked like a burned steak? The marines had a sense that maybe, just maybe, the landing would go off more easily than they expected.

They could not have been more wrong.

H HOUR (THE TIME FOR THE ACTUAL LANDING) was set for 9:00 a.m. on the dot. At 9:02, two minutes behind schedule, the first landing craft hit the beach.

As Kuribayashi had predicted, the landing point was the beach on the south coast of the island. The Japanese allowed the landing operation to go ahead without offering the slightest resistance. Only after 10 a.m., when the beach was jam-packed with marines, supplies, and munitions, did they start their attack. Shells and gunfire rained down onto the beach, while antiaircraft guns and artillery, their barrels lowered, began to pick off the landing craft.

It was *funshinhô*—rocket guns—that wreaked the greatest havoc. They fired self-propelled shells, and unlike large pieces of artillery, they did not need large launching frames so they could be transported and assembled with ease. The Japanese had been using rocket guns in combat in the South Seas since 1943. They were among the most deadly and effective weapons that Kuribayashi was given by the military central command, and they were a major factor in the robust resistance of the Iwo Jima garrison.

The black sand on the southern beaches was soft volcanic cinders, and the ground was broken into a series of terraces. The marines who had come ashore sank in up to their ankles with every step they took, and with their feet bogging down in sand with the texture of coffee beans, getting beyond the terraces proved difficult. The beach looked like rush hour with all the marines milling about.

Artillery fire came cascading down on them relentlessly. The beach offered no cover and digging trenches was impossible. The Americans could move neither forward nor back, and the casualties mounted. Such was the power of the rocket guns that a direct hit would literally blow someone to bits. The gruesome carnage struck terror into the Americans, and for a short time the beach was a scene of panic and chaos.

Kuribayashi's strategy—allowing the Americans to land before picking them off from close quarters rather than clinging to the old orthodoxy of stopping the enemy from coming ashore—proved itself effective. On that single day, 566 American soldiers were killed or missing in action; 1,755 were wounded; and 99 were so traumatized that they could fight no more. This adds up to 8 percent of the total 31,000-man-strong landing force.

The Japanese side sustained heavy damage, too. The defenses at the water's edge were put almost completely out of action on the first day (though their loss was already factored in). Kuribayashi never planned on a showdown at the water's edge; his aim was to inflict as much damage as he could, then continue to resist from his main inland defenses, before finally holing up in the honeycomb position.

The sun set on D-Day at 6:45 p.m., but night did not mean sleep for the exhausted marines: they had no way of knowing when the banzai charge might come.

The Americans were sure there would be a large-scale banzai charge on the day they landed. It had been that way on every other Pacific island they had invaded up to this point. Officers brandishing Japanese swords, soldiers armed with bayonets and grenades, the sound of strange voices, howls, cry after cry of "banzai." Although the

Americans hated and feared these attacks, they also represented an opportunity to dramatically reduce the fighting power of the Japanese. The Japanese soldiers who charged in so recklessly were always equally quickly slaughtered.

The combination of casualties from the fighting on the beach by day and the banzai charge at night usually meant that the fighting ability of the Japanese would fall sharply on the first day of any battle. That was the basis of the Americans' conviction that Iwo Jima would fall in five days.

Early morning on D-day plus one (the day after the landing), Lieutenant General Smith was on the deck of the *Eldorado*, gazing at the island and wondering why the Japanese had not yet made their banzai charge. Smith did not yet know what kind of man the commander in chief of Iwo Jima was.

Kuribayashi's battle was only just getting started.

WHAT WAS KURIBAYASHI THINKING in the battle command post in the Command Center when the Americans came ashore?

Accounts written by American historians tend to paint a picture of Kuribayashi, the consummate samurai warrior, biding his time, ready to pounce on the enemy. But what was really passing through his mind?

"America is the last country in the world Japan should fight."

This was something Kuribayashi had told his family repeatedly before the outbreak of war. His opinion derived from the time he had spent in the United States and the evidence of the power of the country he had seen with his own eyes. "It was because His Lordship the General was opposed to starting a war against the United States that Prime Minister Tôjô disliked him and ordered him off to Iwo Jima." This is still the opinion of Sadaoka Nobuyoshi, the former army civilian employee.

The United States may also have been "the most difficult country" for Kuribayashi to fight. After all, in the course of his two-year sojourn there while in his thirties, Kuribayashi had not just experienced the industrial and military power of the place, but the everyday life of the people—and they were just like the Japanese.

When I first visited Tarô Kuribayashi's house in Akishima in the fall of 2003, I was shown one folder of letters that did not come from Iwo Jima. Reading them, I was surprised at how different they were from the letters he had sent from the front.

Each letter was a brief passage of text coupled with humorous and deftly drawn illustrations on unlined white paper. There were forty-two letters in total. Kuribayashi had written them to his family while he was studying in the United States.

I felt I had stumbled upon an unlikely talent for Kuribayashi to have. The drawings were all surprisingly good: there was nothing amateurish about their freedom and confidence of line.

Tarô, Kuribayashi's son, was three at the time and not yet able to read. It was for him that Kuribayashi described, on August 27, 1928, from Buffalo, New York, his life in America in pictures.

> *This is an American child*
> *At play*
> *Here tricycles are all the rage*
> *And when your daddy sees*
> *Children playing that way*
> *I always stand rooted to the spot a while*
> *And look at them*
> *Thinking: I wonder if little Tarô*
> *Is having fun playing like this, too?*

The letter includes a pen drawing of a group of three children playing on tricycles.

Off in a foreign land, Kuribayashi must have often thought about his young son, as little children make frequent appearances in his illustrated letters, whether he's giving a child a lift back from school in a car, or admiring the dancing of the daughter of an army captain friend. Kuribayashi would even invite the newspaper delivery boy in for a meal, or talk to a couple of poor brothers out on the street at night.

Daddy has invited in the delivery boy
And given him a slap-up meal

He has a stepmother now, not a mother
His real mother
Died when he was just a baby
So he never knew her
"My daddy is a sergeant-major
He works in a place called 'the accounts room'
Do you know him, Mister?
When I get bigger, I'll go to Japan, sure I will
So your son's called Tarô, Mister?
Reckon that's an interesting name . . ."

"Ah, I see
Are you tired out from delivering the papers every night?
It's all right. Today I bought candy and walnuts
All sorts of nice things for you
So go on then, eat up
What? Me, teach you Japanese?
It's difficult, you know."

At about nine at night
Daddy gets out of his car and walks a little
In a murky spot, standing dejectedly,
Were two children
One of them was of the same age as Tarô

Without thinking I stopped in my tracks
"What are you doing out so late?
Are you brothers?
Where are your shoes? What? You haven't got any?
Poor you. I'll give you both a little bit of money. . . ."

"This is my little brother
Yes, we are Mexicans
Our father drinks too much and life's difficult
Me, I'm six
Our father doesn't give us any money at all
Thank you. Thank you. Thank you."

The illustrated letters were neatly bound like a book. By the time I looked at them, more than seventy-five years had passed since they were written, but they were neither stained nor damaged, and the two illustrations that had been colored in had not faded at all. It was obvious that the family had preserved them with the greatest care.

Tarô was reluctant to talk much about the letters from Iwo Jima— the scene of his father's death—but his expression softened when he looked at the illustrated letters. In them his father is a young man, overflowing with curiosity, hope, and ambition, while Japan has yet to plunge into a doomed war. In light of what the family was later to experience, this was a happy time for them, even though duty had taken the head of the family abroad.

"It looks like my father was a big hit in America. Here, have a look at this one."

Tarô was pointing at a letter in which a group of people were waving good-bye to Kuribayashi as he went off in a taxi. When he started his studies in America, he lodged with an ordinary, nonmilitary family in Buffalo, New York. The picture shows him leaving Buffalo to go to Washington, D.C., from where, on November 19, 1928, he had written:

> *My landlady in Buffalo*
> *And all the ladies of the neighborhood*
> *Are sorry*
> *That Daddy is leaving*
> *That's how much Daddy*
> *Was loved by them all.*

Kuribayashi had sailed for America in March 1928. He was a thirty-six-year-old cavalry captain five years out of the Army War College.

Overseas study was a special privilege of the *guntô-gumi,* the "saber squad," officers who had graduated with honors from the Army War College and were so named because they were personally presented with a saber by the emperor. Members of the saber squad would go to countries like Germany, Russia, Great Britain, the United States, and China to study, with Germany being the most popular destination.

Kuribayashi was in the twenty-sixth graduating class of the Military Academy. An examination of the overseas destinations selected by the twenty-eight graduates from the twenty-fifth, twenty-sixth, and twenty-seventh classes shows that Germany, chosen by ten people, was top, with France, chosen by seven, in second place. The unpopularity of English-speaking countries is striking, with only four graduates choosing the United States, and one choosing Great Britain.

There were few people in the Japanese army who knew much about Great Britain or the United States, and the resulting tendency to underestimate their military and industrial might was to prove one of the causes behind Japan's defeat in the Pacific War. This deficiency was directly related to the army's system for educating its high-level officers.

The typical course followed by elite army officers involved Military Preparatory School, followed by the Military Academy, and culminating in graduation from the Army War College. It was also possible to attend an ordinary middle school (under the old system) rather than the Military Preparatory School, and go on to the Military Academy.

Graduates of the Military Preparatory School, however, fared far better when it came to promotion. The idea was deeply entrenched that the graduates of the Military Preparatory School were privileged, while anyone who had graduated from an ordinary middle school was merely acceptable. As a result, most of the pivotal posts in the army were held by officers who had attended the Military Preparatory School.

The foreign language curriculum at the Military Preparatory School included German, French, and Russian, with English not offered until 1938. Since the Japanese army was modeled on the German army, the majority of students chose to learn German. This also accounted for the large numbers of army men who chose to do their overseas study in Germany.

In ordinary middle schools, however, English was compulsory. Many of the young officers who had progressed to the Military Academy from such schools chose to spend their period of overseas study in English-speaking countries like the United States and Great Britain. But since the products of ordinary middle schools were not viewed very highly, officers with a strong knowledge of the United States and Great Britain seldom attained the most important posts.

Kuribayashi was not a product of the Military Preparatory School, having progressed to the Military Academy via a middle school in Nagano. One of Kuribayashi's men from the days when he had commanded the First Cavalry Brigade in Baotou, China, told me that he believed "Kuribayashi having not gone to the Military Preparatory School was a major factor in his having such a breadth of vision."

Army officers who had attended the Military Preparatory School were often criticized for having an overweening sense of being "special" and also a narrow way of thinking. The Military Preparatory School had been modeled on the Prussian schools that turned the sons of the aristocracy into soldiers, and high-ranking officers often sent their sons to the school.

Kuribayashi, good at English thanks to graduating from an ordinary middle school, chose to study in the United States. He went off alone, leaving his wife and son behind in Japan. Attached to the U.S. First Cavalry Division for military study, Kuribayashi found the time to audit courses at Harvard University and the University of Michigan, where he studied English, American history, and U.S. current affairs.

Kuribayashi was fascinated by the motorization boom in the United States. He acquired a Chevrolet K, a state-of-the-art model at the time, learned how to drive it, and in December 1929 had an "adventure," driving it the entire 1,300 kilometers from Kansas to Washington, D.C. His illustrated letters depict all the difficulties he encountered on his journey, including crossing mountains on narrow, snow-covered roads and getting a tire puncture in the middle of a snowstorm.

In a letter to his eldest brother, Kuribayashi recounts a surprising experience he had during this trip when his car broke down, leaving him stranded. A girl of seventeen or eighteen who happened to drive by—herself at the wheel—repaired his car. Kuribayashi was most impressed that in the United States anyone over sixteen with the right paperwork was allowed to drive, and that everyone was able to perform routine maintenance themselves.

It was from everyday experiences like this—and not just from book learning—that Kuribayashi developed a sense of the economic gulf separating the United States and Japan. The United States was a place where "the housekeeper lady" who looked after Kuribayashi could also own her own car.

> *The housekeeper lady has recently*
> *Bought herself a new car*
> *And is showing it to Daddy*

> *"I see*
> *I see*

I see
That's great
If you take good care of it
It will last a good long time."

"Hey, captain
I just bought myself this new car
It cost me 400 dollars
It's an old model, so they gave me a good price.
The old one? I gave it to my husband.

I keep separate accounts from him
My husband is a genuinely good man
But he likes to drink and gamble
And I don't like it when he nags me for money
Even since the beginning of this year, I've lent him so much
Chitter-chatter-chitter-chatter blah-blah-blah-blah."

What Daddy was thinking was:
An automobile like this
Is much better than the buses
Running in the Japanese countryside
Japan has got to pull itself together. . . .
That, and her keeping her money separate from her husband,
It's so typically American. . . .

Kuribayashi started on his way home in April 1930, but as he made stops in London, Paris, and Berlin, he only got back to Japan in July.

In the course of his two-year stint in America, Kuribayashi had socialized with American military men and their families, and he counted some of them as true friends. One of them was Brigadier General George Van Horn Moseley, the head of the U.S. Army Cavalry School.

At the Kuribayashi house, I was shown the photograph album covering his years in America. It included a portrait of Brigadier General Moseley, with the inscription: "With high regard and esteem. I shall never forget our happy association together in America. Best wishes to you and to Japan."

While Kuribayashi waited for the Americans to come ashore, deep in his underground bunker surrounded by the stench of sulfur, did he think about the newspaper delivery boy, about driving in his Chevrolet, or about the families of the soldiers who had invited him into their homes?

February 19, 1945; D-day. Kuribayashi was trapped in one of the ironies of history, about to engage the United States—the country he least wanted to fight—in battle at the front line of his Japanese homeland.

CHAPTER SEVEN

THE ISLAND WHERE YOU WALK ON THE DEAD

—

"IF YOU LOOK OUT OF THE WINDOW ON THE RIGHT, IWO JIMA WILL soon be coming into view."

When a crew member made this announcement, everyone undid their seat belts and got out of their seats. Two and a half hours had passed since the Air Self-Defense Force C-1 transport plane had lifted off from Iruma Air Base in Saitama Prefecture.

The transport plane had only a few modestly sized portholes. Taking turns to peer out of them were members of the families of the Japanese soldiers who had died fighting on the island.

I placed my forehead against the faintly misted glass and looked down. The island was small enough to fit inside the small round window only 50 centimeters across.

"Such a tiny place," whispered an old woman beside me as she leaned on her cane. She had been holding a bunch of white flowers to her chest ever since we took off at Iruma.

We only started our descent after slowly circling the island many times, as though to give the families time to burn its image onto their retinas.

"Did you know that there are bones of the dead sleeping under the runway? When we disembark from the plane, we will be walking on the dead."

The man who said this to me was in late middle age. His father had died on Iwo Jima.

I had heard about the bones beneath the runway from many people. The present Self-Defense Force airfield is located on the site of the Japanese forces' wartime Motoyama Airfield. When the Americans captured the airfield, it was littered with the corpses of the Japanese soldiers who had fought to the death defending it. In their haste to repair and enlarge the runway for the conquest of the Japanese homeland, the Americans reportedly left the bodies uncollected and spread asphalt directly on top of them.

When the Ogasawara Islands, of which Iwo Jima is a part, were returned to Japan, the Self-Defense Force took over the airfield and constructed a new runway in a slightly different location from the American one. At that time, emergency digs were carried out in thirty-three locations in one area and as many of the dead as possible were recovered, but the remains of many others are still thought to be buried beneath it.

There, where their fathers, husbands, and brothers died, the families have no choice but to walk upon the bones of the dead. That is Iwo Jima.

The Self-Defense Force is not alone in making use of the runway; carrier-based U.S. planes also practice nighttime take-offs and landings there. Since no one lives on the island, there is no one to protest the noise, and as Iwo Jima is far out to sea and free from artificial light, the airfield makes a perfect stand-in for an aircraft carrier out on the high seas. Planes of both the Japanese Self-Defense Force and the American military are thus constantly taking off and landing on top of the remains of Japanese soldiers.

The thought is enough to make you tremble as you step off the plane, but if you stop to think about it, this is not the only place on the island where there are bones of Japanese soldiers. After all, 95 percent of the more than twenty thousand Japanese soldiers who fought on Iwo

Jima died in the battle. Most of the one thousand or so who survived to become prisoners of war were seriously wounded and were taken care of by the U.S. forces.

Methodical collecting of the remains has been conducted since 1970, but the remains of more than thirteen thousand men are still lying beneath the earth. No matter where you are, the very act of walking on the island is to walk upon the dead.

The bones of Kuribayashi himself may be among them. It was then standard practice for the general to commit hara-kiri behind the lines during the final all-out attack that ended in death, but Kuribayashi broke this custom, too, when he led his men himself.

Impressed by the courage of the enemy general, the Americans tried to find his corpse once the battle was over, but could not since the Japanese had all removed the insignia from their uniforms. Kuribayashi chose the anonymous sleep of death somewhere in the depths of the island—just like the men he commanded.

IT WAS DECEMBER 2004 when I accompanied the families on their one-day memorial pilgrimage.

Proper memorial visits for the families of the dead started in the early 1970s. Different commemorative rites are conducted on Iwo Jima, but the organizer of the pilgrimage in which I took part was the Association of Iwo Jima, while a representative from the Ministry of Health, Labour and Welfare (the government department with oversight for such matters) came with us, and the Self-Defense Force provided assistance. Battle survivors and families of the dead established the Association of Iwo Jima in 1953, and this nongovernmental group has been diligently collecting the remains of the dead and organizing memorial activities ever since.

Present-day Iwo Jima has no real inhabitants. There are around 350 people from the Maritime and Air Self-Defense Forces permanently stationed there, plus a handful of staff from the Defense Facilities Administration Agency and construction company employees on the island for building projects.

The population was compulsorily evacuated in the summer of 1944, the year before the Americans invaded, to protect them from the horrors of war, and they were not permitted to return to the island even after it was returned to Japan. It was decided that a permanent settlement would be too difficult to maintain, given that the island has no industry of its own, and that fresh food and most other necessities have to be imported.

In consequence, there are no private houses on present-day Iwo Jima, nor, aside from a little kiosk inside the Self-Defense Force facility, is there a single shop. Families and people with a special connection to the dead are allowed to visit the island on memorial pilgrimages, and the former inhabitants are allowed to visit family graves. Otherwise ordinary people are technically not permitted to set foot on the place. The whole island really is a military base now.

The Japanese military ordered that Iwo Jima be defended to the death because it was an "unsinkable aircraft carrier" on the Pacific Ocean. That designation may be even more appropriate now when there is nothing there apart from the airfield and the facilities that go with it.

After disembarking from the plane, the families climbed into a number of cars and headed to the northeast corner of the island, where the Tenzan Memorial stands.

The paved road that runs around the island is surrounded by greenery, but maybe because Iwo Jima is a volcanic island where the smell of sulfur always hangs in the air—or maybe because of the strong salt breeze that blows nonstop from the sea—there is none of the luxuriant jungle one associates with South Sea islands, just masses of stunted, shrublike trees.

The Americans are supposed to have fired so many shells and bombs into the island that the total volume of metal would cover the island in a steel sheet one meter thick. All of the island's animal and plant life was incinerated, and now the most flourishing plant on the island is the lead tree, a kind of arborescent shrub.

The lead tree is not indigenous to Iwo Jima. After the Americans had captured the island, they spread great quantities of seeds from airplanes. It is suggested that they deliberately chose a plant that takes root and grows quickly in order to wipe out the stench from the exposed corpses of the Japanese soldiers.

A memorial service was held on Tenzan, a small hill exposed to the strong winds that blow in from the sea. One after another, the family members walked up to the memorial stone to douse it with water that they had brought with them from their hometowns in canteens or plastic bottles.

Fifty family members took part. The widows were from their late seventies to their eighties; the youngest of the children of the dead was a woman of fifty-nine who had still been in her mother's womb when her father went off to war.

The participants also included people who were not strictly family.

"My husband died ten years ago. He was transferred from here back to the mainland before the Americans invaded, and right up until he died he was tortured by the fact that he survived while almost all the men under him were killed. My husband always said that he wanted to come here to pay his respects, but was unable to fulfill his wish. That's why my daughter and I are here today."

The wife was seventy-seven years old, the daughter fifty-two. They had brought a photograph of their husband/father with them and they spent a long time in prayer in front of the memorial.

We then climbed back into the station wagons and microbuses and headed for the interior of the island. In advance, the Association of Iwo

Jima had checked the whereabouts on the island of the men who had died based on which part of Japan they came from and the names of their units.

The family members all asked if they could visit the places where their relatives had died to offer incense and prayer, but time was limited as our return plane was due to leave a little after 4:00 p.m.

Covered in shrubs and weeds, Iwo Jima appears flat at first glance, but as it is a volcanic island the terrain is extremely uneven. A single misstep can mean a nasty fall—the bunkers themselves are often concealed. In some rocky areas, steam spewing out at high temperatures means that venturing off the paved road is dangerous.

Even if you knew that the unit to which your husband, father, or brother belonged was stationed just a little way away, getting in closer was forbidden; only paying homage from the roadside or from inside the car was permitted.

"Please, let me get closer. Thirty seconds is all I need. Let me get out of the car to offer incense."

I could hear voices imploring the driver, an older man dressed in a very proper suit despite the beating sun. The voices contained sixty years' worth of grief—the grief of people who had at long last made it to the place where their relatives had died.

KURIBAYASHI'S COMMAND BUNKER was situated in the north of the island.

He chose this place as the site of his final resistance on the assumption that the Americans would work their way up the island from south to north, which was precisely what happened. The bunker is at the extreme tip of the island: to the north there is only the shore running from Onsen Hama to Kita no Hana.

Surrounded by higher ground, the bunker nestles within a horseshoe-shaped rise. The entrance is visible at the base of the low bluff of light brown rock. You would need to stoop a little to go inside. At the time, of course, it would have been thoroughly camouflaged.

I peered in, but couldn't see far into the dark cave; a few rusty steel rods stuck out of the cement still framing the doorway in places. The ground underfoot was slippery and sloped downward, leading to a flight of stairs. After going down them a while, the passageway suddenly grew much smaller. I was walking hunched and with my knees bent but my back was still scraping on the roof. No light from outside reached this far inside, and moving forward without a flashlight was out of the question.

After I had walked a few meters, the passage made a sharp turn to the left and led to a small room with a floor area equivalent to about six tatami mats. Sturdily built and reinforced with concrete, this was Kuribayashi's private room.

Kuribayashi had commanded from here, right from the start of the softening-up campaign of naval barrages and air raids that preceded the invasion. It was here that he refined his strategy, listened to the reports from the units on different parts of the island, issued his orders, and drafted the reports and telegrams that were sent to the Imperial General Headquarters. There was nothing in the room now and it was bleak and empty, but in those days there must have been a desk for Kuribayashi to work at.

There is a story that an American soldier armed with a flamethrower penetrated as far as the door of this room when the Americans were bearing down on the Command Center in early March 1945.

Kuribayashi, however, was so focused on his work that he didn't notice and just continued poring over the documents on his desk. The sentry quickly unfurled a military-issue blanket to act as a screen between the American soldier and his commander in chief. "Oh, thanks," said Kuribayashi, rising to his feet and calmly walking farther into the cave. Overawed by this display of nerve, the American soldier turned on his heel and fled.

The Japanese soldiers recounted this story to one another as an example of Kuribayashi's courage. It is not clear whether the episode really occurred, but the fact that the story spread by word of mouth in the midst of combat reveals how Kuribayashi was seen by his men: as a splendid commanding officer for whom they were willing to die. The boost such feelings gave them must have gone some way to help them accept the inevitability of death.

Leaving Kuribayashi's room and proceeding farther down the passageway I suddenly emerged into a big space. The roof was probably around 3 meters high and had half crumbled away to expose the rock beneath. A natural cave that had been enlarged, it felt more like an enormous cellar than a room; supposedly it was used for strategy meetings.

Leading off from the cave in all four directions were passages. Niches just big enough for a single person to lie down had been carved into the walls. You can no longer go down these passages—some are impassable and others have been blocked off with iron bars—but they crisscrossed like a veritable maze and were connected to nine separate entrances and exits.

Kuribayashi's letters to his family before the American invasion were probably written aboveground rather than down here, but the farewell telegram, the last thing he ever wrote, must have been written here in the Command Center. In the same small and precisely drawn characters and with the same writing paper and pencil that he used for the letters to his family, Kuribayashi composed that telegram here deep underground where the sun could not reach.

After the guide had left, I stood in the center of Kuribayashi's private room and turned off my flashlight. Suddenly the air felt thick, and the darkness seemed to press heavily down on me from the roof of the cave. Had Kuribayashi ever left the cave to feel the sun on his skin in the thirty-six days between the American landing and the defeat of the

Japanese? It is believed that it was early on March 26 that Kuribayashi led the final all-out attack. Had it still been dark then?

Even after the Japanese had been defeated and the Americans had occupied the island, many Japanese soldiers continued hiding out in the defenses and waged a guerrilla war against the Americans. Under cover of night, they would strike at American defenses or forage for food and water. In the daylight hours, they would hide underground, so they were not exposed to the sun for many days, even months.

Survivors told me how, their minds blurred and their bodies no more than skin and bone, as food and water started to run out, they would suddenly get the urge to see the sun before they died, even though it meant that they would be captured as they crawled out of their shelters and so become prisoners of war. Many, however, were trapped belowground and either suffocated or starved to death after the Americans blasted the entrances of the caves they were in.

If you go deep into one of the caves, it doesn't take long before the oppressive darkness and the heavy, stagnant air make you feel panicky.

I remembered the telegram sent by Rear Admiral Ichimaru Rinosuke, commander of the navy forces: "The enemy are aboveground and friendly troops belowground: that is what is unusual about the battle on Iwo Jima." And once again I felt keenly just how pitiless a strategy Kuribayashi had chosen.

NOBODY KNOWS HOW MANY underground bunkers were built on Iwo Jima: the number is thought to exceed one thousand, with some historians putting the figure as high as five thousand. Many of the bunkers still remain undiscovered—along with the bones inside them. During the battle, and directly after the capture of the island, the Americans blasted shut the cave entrances or buried entire positions with bulldozers. By the time Iwo Jima was returned to the Japanese it was therefore difficult to pinpoint where things were, and the search is now further complicated by the vegetation that covers the island.

When they started collecting the remains of the dead, the survivors relied partly on memory to find the bunkers in which they had hidden, and partly on the meager extant documentation. The present method involves hacking out a path through the branches of the lead trees and the creeping plants entwined around them, and crawling on hands and knees to find the bunker entrances. Sometimes bulldozers are used to push the upper layer of earth aside and dig out the bunker below. Occasionally, if they find one of the blasting fuses the Americans used to pay out when blowing the bunkers shut, they can follow these until they find the bunker entrance.

The bunkers themselves are often half full of earth. This earth is carefully extracted and sieved to check for remains. Sometimes the dead are almost perfectly preserved.

On the pilgrimage I went on, there was a man who had been orphaned in the war and was visiting the island for the third time. His name was Yamagiwa Yoshikazu, and he and his wife had traveled from Oita Prefecture. His father had died on Iwo Jima. Called up at the age of thirty-nine, he had three children, of whom Yamagiwa, then at elementary school, was the eldest. His widowed mother went through great hardship after the war bringing up three children all by herself, he told me.

In 1984, Yamagiwa had taken part in a visit to collect the remains of the dead. This was in the early days when the practice of families going out and gathering first began in earnest. In the course of about four weeks, they collected the remains of 135 people.

"The caves had been sealed tightly shut for forty years, so there was no oxygen in them. The first thing we did was use a machine to pump in oxygen. Then we roped ourselves up and were lowered down, dangling from the surface. The first cave I went into was 20 meters deep."

No one is allowed to work inside a cave for more than twenty minutes, Yamagiwa told me, as there are places where the temperature can be as high as 176 degrees Fahrenheit—not to mention the danger of being poisoned by sulfur gas

Sometimes they could see the bones of the dead, but extreme heat or lack of oxygen prevented them from collecting them, and the sense of guilt made them weep long and hard. The families do not distinguish between the bones of relations and nonrelations. For them, everyone is equal.

When he first started, Yamagiwa told me that he used to wear army-issue cotton gloves for the work, but it was not long before he began to pick up the bones with his bare hands.

"If you've got army-issue cotton gloves on, any bones you pick up stick to your hands."

The bones of someone who has been cremated are smooth, but the bones of a corpse that's been abandoned and has gone through the process of natural decay are sticky. That is the reason the bones stick fast to gloves. For Yamagiwa, it felt as though the bones were stubbornly refusing to let go of the hand of the person who had at long last come from the homeland to collect them.

Yamagiwa explained to me that there are white bones and black bones in the caves. The white bones belong either to men who were killed by bombs and bullets, or to those who got progressively weaker and died. The black bones belong to the men who were burned to death by flamethrowers.

Contemporary newsreels and photographs convey the awesome power of the American flamethrowers, which were able to turn a broad swath of ground into a sea of fire. The Americans also poured a mixture of gasoline and seawater into the bunkers, lit it, and roasted the soldiers within to death.

On the beach at the northern tip of the island, Yamagiwa and the rest of the group cremated the 135 sets of remains they had collected.

"They died out here so far to the south. We thought that cremating them even that much closer to the homeland was the least we could do."

All of the participants had watched the fire burn throughout the night. Any bones that were left were placed in plain wood boxes and taken back to the homeland, while the remaining ashes were carefully hand-collected before being scattered into the sea.

"We tried to find a current that was flowing to the north for them. We stood on the beach for a long time, all of us shouting: 'Go on now. Go on back to your homeland.' "

AFTER VISITING SEVERAL PLACES where engagements had occurred and a number of bunkers, we headed for Mount Suribachi, on the southern tip of the island. The road that leads to the summit follows the path the Americans took when they climbed up, clearing the way with their flamethrowers.

Mount Suribachi stands only 169 meters above sea level, but since there are no other mountains or uplands, you can take in the entire island from its summit. I use the word "summit," but as the mountain is a dormant volcano I'm actually talking about the lip of the north side of the deep crater, an area only about the size of a soccer pitch.

On D-day plus four, a group of U.S. Marines raised the Stars and Stripes in this place, and the photograph of the event became famous as the "most beautiful picture of the war." Just in front of where the base of the original flagpole stood, there now stands the American Armed Forces Victory Memorial, which was erected when the island was under American occupation.

A copperplate of the Stars and Stripes and a bas-relief of the marines raising the flag stand upon a white pedestal, and on either side are two V shapes, perhaps representing "victory."

I noticed clusters of small pieces of metal clinging to the V-shaped parts of the memorial. I went up to have a closer look and they turned out to be chains with oval disks on them. Hundreds of them were hanging there.

They are identification tags stamped with tiny numbers and letters belonging to U.S. Marines. American soldiers wear these metal tags marked with their name and rank so as to identify them if they're killed in action. These identification tags must be worn not just in combat, for training, or for maneuvers, but all the time.

Many of the marines who now come to Iwo Jima for training hang their identification tags on the memorial to honor the dead before they leave the island. The marines are proud to be a part of the same tradition as their predecessors who fought on the island some sixty years ago, and even now Iwo Jima remains holy ground for them.

The Medal of Honor is a decoration awarded in recognition of extraordinary acts of valor on the battlefield. During the four years of World War II, the marines earned a total of eighty-four Medals of Honor. Twenty-seven of these were awarded for the action on Iwo Jima—almost one third for a battle that lasted thirty-six days. This statistic alone shows why Iwo Jima is a battle that lives on in history.

Draped in hundreds of identification tags, the victory monument is inscribed with the words of Admiral Nimitz: "Among the Americans who served on IWO JIMA, uncommon valor was a common virtue."

Of the six soldiers who raised the flag on Mount Suribachi, three were killed in the subsequent fighting. The remaining three returned in triumph to their homeland, where they were fêted as heroes and made to take part in a campaign to sell war bonds to help cover the cost of the war.

The American people gave them a wildly enthusiastic welcome at every stop of their national tour and purchased $26.3 billion worth of war bonds during that one summer. It was a sum equivalent to almost half the entire government budget for 1946.

A commemorative stamp with the photograph of the marines raising the flag was issued in July, less than four months after the battle itself ended. It was the first time in American history that living people had been featured on a stamp. One hundred and fifty million copies of the stamp were sold.

In 1954 the photograph was turned into the world's tallest bronze statue, which went up in Arlington National Cemetery. The entire $850,000 cost was covered by donations from ordinary people.

The American people were first horrified at the casualties on Iwo Jima, then ecstatic at the hard-won victory, and the battle remains deeply engraved on the public consciousness even now. This explains why Kuribayashi, the man who was considered to have made America suffer more than anyone, may be better known in the United States than in Japan.

In May 2003, U.S. President George W. Bush made a speech declaring the end of major combat operations in Iraq. In it, he praised the military, saying: "The daring of Normandy, the fierce courage of Iwo Jima . . . is fully present in this generation." Even after the passage of more than half a century, Iwo Jima remains a symbol of courage and victory for the United States.

A MEMORIAL ERECTED by the Japanese also stands on top of Mount Suribachi. The monument erected by the Americans commemorates their victory, but the Japanese monument is designed to commemorate and console their dead.

It is made of black granite, heavy and solid, and features a map of Japan made with stones from all the prefectures of the nation representing all the soldiers who fought at Iwo Jima, who came from almost every part of the country.

The greater part of the Japanese soldiers—officers and men—who fought on Iwo Jima were not career soldiers, but ordinary people: farmers, shopkeepers, businessmen, teachers, and student conscripts. They were people living normal lives who were drafted and dispatched to the island.

Carved on the top left of the map is the phrase *Iô-Jima Senbotsusha Kenshôhi*—"Monument to the Honor of the Fallen of Iwo Jima." The stone itself was erected precisely one year after the island was restored to Japan.

As you stand there on the summit with the two memorials side by side—one commemorating victory, the other the ordinary lives that were lost—the south beach where the Americans landed looks so close you feel as though you could reach out and touch it.

It was in 1985, forty years after the war, that the south beach hosted the "Reunion of Honor."

This was an event that brought together Japanese and American veterans, former friend and former foe alike. Its aim was twofold: to commemorate the fallen on both sides, and to swear peace to each other. Nowhere else have the participants in a battle that was so cruel, and that claimed so many lives, held a reunion ceremony on the very ground where they fought. But such an event took place on Iwo Jima. Including family members, a total of almost four hundred people—both Japanese and American—took part.

There is a striking scene in the video documentary made that day. The American and Japanese veterans and their families start out standing in separate groups, but as the ceremony ends, without either side seeming to take the initiative, they start drifting toward one another.

They shake one another's hands, timidly at first, then more forcefully. Weeping, they hug one another and start to make conversation through sign language and gestures. "I still have a bullet in my leg," says one. "I'll betcha I'm the guy who fired it," jokes another. "I had terrible burns on my face and you Americans saved me. My nose is 'Made in the U.S.A.,' " says a Japanese veteran with a grin. Now even the families of the dead have clasped one another's hands.

Not everyone who took part in the reunion did so willingly. The video introduces us to Ed Moranick, who participated in the landing operation as a marine in the 4th Division. There's a scene on the plane heading for Iwo Jima where he says, "This is no pleasure trip for me. When I think how much my wife has suffered. . . . To be honest, the thought of having a reunion with Japanese veterans really depresses me."

On Iwo Jima, Moranick was struck in the face by a shell, and his appearance was completely transformed. In a portrait photograph taken just after the war, his nose is almost completely gone, while his eyes and mouth are significantly deformed. After the war, he needed twenty-two reconstructive surgeries before he could return to normal life.

On the return flight from Iwo Jima, the expression on Moranick's face is different. "Forty years ago I came to this island to kill 'Japs'; I didn't even think of them as 'people,' " he says. "But now I'm sorry that we slaughtered each other like that. Really and truly sorry."

In 1984, a ceremony was also held to commemorate the fortieth anniversary of the Normandy landings, but only the victorious nations— the United States, Great Britain, France, and so on—took part, and the purpose of the ceremony was to commemorate their victory. In this respect, the scenes played out on Iwo Jima were highly unusual.

A joint Japanese-American commemoration ceremony is now held every year. Why is it only at Iwo Jima that men who previously devoted themselves to killing one another have managed to meet and achieve reconciliation like this? Is it because they fought such a savage, all-out battle at such close quarters that now, with the passage of time, they are able to forgive and accept one another? This, I suspect, is something only the people who fought there can really understand.

A memorial was erected on the south beach where the 1985 ceremony was held. It bears the following inscription in both English and Japanese.

ON THE 40TH ANNIVERSARY OF THE BATTLE OF IWO JIMA,
AMERICAN AND JAPANESE VETERANS MET AGAIN ON THESE
SAME SANDS, THIS TIME IN PEACE AND FRIENDSHIP.

WE COMMEMORATE OUR COMRADES, LIVING AND DEAD, WHO
FOUGHT HERE WITH BRAVERY AND HONOR, AND WE PRAY
TOGETHER THAT OUR SACRIFICES ON IWO JIMA WILL
ALWAYS BE REMEMBERED AND NEVER BE REPEATED.
FEBRUARY 19, 1985

3RD, 4TH, 5TH DIVISION ASSOCIATIONS: USMC
AND
THE ASSOCIATION OF IWO JIMA

CHAPTER EIGHT

THE SOLDIERS' LETTERS

—

Kuribayashi encouraged his men to write letters and send money home to their families, so in the months leading up to the American invasion, they diligently wrote home during breaks in their maneuvers and the building of their defensive installations. Many of the families carefully preserve these letters as substitutes for the relics of the dead, as the bones and personal effects of few of the fallen were sent back from Iwo Jima.

The soldiers, for their part, eagerly looked forward to letters from their families. It was the Kisarazu 1023 Flying Corps that exploited the intervals between air raids to bring the letters that served as a link between the hearts of the soldiers and their families. There was always a bundle of letters on these planes, crammed with crew, spare parts, medical supplies and drinking water. The journey was dangerous for transport planes as they were not armed, but the letters and photographs that their families sent were a major source of spiritual strength for the soldiers.

I received the long-awaited photograph of Masayuki safely. I got the letter in a bundle of two or three, but opened this one the minute I saw that the sender's name was Masayuki. He's grown so much. You've done a great job to raise him so plump and healthy.

Thank you. Thank you so much. Keep good care of him from now on, too.

I was so pleased at how cute and clever he looks that I took the photo round to my comrades at the HQ and told them: "Hey, take a look at this picture of my kid." Perhaps they were just being nice, but they said he looked just like me. I quickly tracked down some cardboard and rigged a handy little photo stand, and then I put the picture on the shelf where I look at it every day. I'll probably bore a hole through poor Masayuki any minute!

This is a letter that Kobayashi Issaku of the Second Independent Machine Gun Battalion wrote to his wife. The tenth letter he had sent from the front, it reached her on November 5, 1944.

Masayuki was Kobayashi's first son, who had been born after he had already gone to the front. Ultimately, Kobayashi was to die without ever seeing his son's face outside this photograph. Of the 228 men in his battalion, only one—a medical worker whose movements were different from the rest of the group—survived.

I got the picture with Masayuki and Kuniko snuggling up to each other on the sixteenth. He's grown so big! I literally gasped when I opened the letter and saw the picture. He's so cute it's wicked. The NCOs and my friends tell me that if a father and his child resemble one another, then they'll never have a falling out. I like the last photo you sent me when he's smiling—it was sweet—but he looks rather clever in this one with his mouth clamped shut, too.

If you're not going to make a fuss about children as perfect and as cute as these, then there are no children on this earth who deserve to be spoiled! And you can tell everyone I said that. I made a bag from a scrap of tent material and carry the picture around with me all the time in my pocket. From time to time I take it out and talk to Masayuki.

It was February 18, 1945, when the family received this final postcard. The next day, the Americans landed.

There were many other soldiers like Kobayashi who went into battle carrying a treasured family photograph. Andô Tomiji of the Takano Kensetsu construction company collected the bones and personal effects of the dead on Iwo Jima in 1951 and 1952. In his book *Aa Iô-Jima* (*Ah, Iwo Jima*), Andô described his experiences discovering bodies that had rotted away with letters and photographs on them.

In a cave near Tenzan in the north, I found a body. He was just a skeleton with a photograph of his family and a letter pushed into his breast pocket. There were three photographs inside the letter. The blood had soaked into them, but I could still make out a faint image of his mother and brothers.

The corpse was that of a special officer cadet who had graduated from the Utsunomiya Flight School, and the letter was from his mother. Andô continues: "It was a sweet letter full of concern for her son. I am sure the cadet cried out for the mother he saw in his dreams when he dozed off in his dismal defense post."

At the time, special officer cadets could volunteer from the age of fifteen and would be sent off to the front after a brief period of training. This particular cadet was either sixteen or seventeen.

The Japanese soldiers who fought on Iwo Jima came from a broad age range. As the war approached its end, it was getting difficult to find young and healthy men to conscript. As a result, many of the soldiers were middle-aged and had wives and children. Andô also found bodies that were clutching photographs of children.

In the depths of a cave near "Lieutenant General Kuribayashi's Headquarters," there was a father who had died a sad death with a photograph of his beloved child in his chest pocket.

A letter had also survived underneath the pitiful corpse on which scraps of rotting clothing still hung. The faded image of his child was visible in the photograph in the threadbare pocket; the letter itself was clumsily written with Japanese characters as big as your thumb in places.

Near another body Andô found a letter that a second-year elementary school student had written to his father.

Father, are you well so far away at the front? Even with you away, I'm not the tiniest bit lonely. I am studying very hard and mean to grow up into a good person. I heard from Mother that the place you are is a really nice warm place. She said you even have lots of those "banana" things! Lucky you, able to eat papayas and pineapples and other strange fruits. Mother also said that there is not enough water there, which is bad. Please take care of your health and I wish you good luck. I hope you can do your public duty cheerfully. This is what Mother and I ask God for every day.

The transport flights that brought the letters were like a narrow thread connecting the front line to home. It was on February 11, Empire Day, that the thread was cut, ratcheting up the tension and indicating that the American landing was imminent.

"From today there will be no more post." How must the soldiers have felt when they heard that announcement?

IN FEBRUARY 2005, I was lent a scrapbook by the widow of a noncommissioned officer who had died on Iwo Jima.

The owner of the scrapbook was ninety-two-year-old Egawa Mitsue. "You can borrow this if you think it might be helpful," she had said when she handed it to me as I was leaving her home in Iwakuni, Yamaguchi Prefecture.

Her husband, Egawa Masaharu, was drafted at the age of forty-four when he was working as deputy director of the Matsuyamachi branch of Sumitomo Bank in Osaka. He had briefly served in the army in his twenties and was sent to the front as a second lieutenant based on this experience, making him a *Shôshû Shôkô*, or "draftee officer." The fact that a man in his forties should be conscripted shows just how desperate things were at this time.

The words "From the Front" were written on the scrapbook's cover. Mitsue told me that after the war she had pasted into it every postcard her husband had sent her from the front, but when I opened it to look, the first page contained something different.

"These four letters are the last letters my eldest son and I wrote to my husband. They were returned to us undelivered."

The letters were dated February 11 and February 12, 1945, while the postmarks from the Kisarazu Post Office were the thirteenth and fourteenth. The postal service to Iwo Jima had already been canceled by this time, but the families had no way of knowing that.

The last undelivered letter that Mitsue wrote to her husband talked about their three children, aged eight, six, and four, before ending like this:

> *Looking at their sleeping faces, I thought to myself, "Ah, how lucky I am." Who wouldn't be grateful to be blessed with three such beautiful beings? I will do my very best to bring them up to be good little children who will make you happy. I wish you could see what their life is like day to day. Let's write as much as we can.*

I turned the letter over. A label was stuck over the name of the addressee. "Not known at this address," it said.

The three other letters were the same. "Not known at this address":

For the families back at home, this cold phrase must have been devastating.

In the margin of the page, Mitsue had written: "The letters I sent to the front started being returned to me undelivered. I grew more and more worried." When the letters were returned to her, Mitsue did not even know where her husband was fighting.

In those days, the soldiers' families never knew where they had been sent. When family members sent letters to Iwo Jima, they addressed them "Care of Kisarazu Post Office, Chiba Prefecture," followed by the Japanese character for "Courage," which was a sort of code sign indicating the 109th Division, and the name of the unit. From the letters they received, they could guess that their menfolk were somewhere in the South Seas, but they had no way of knowing precisely where.

Mitsue only discovered that her husband had been on Iwo Jima when she received the official report of his death—two years after he had gone to the front, and nine months after the war had ended. Up until then she had gone through the chaos of the immediate postwar period with the burden of three children while not even knowing if her husband was dead or alive.

A woman in her thirties who had heard that I was researching the battle of Iwo Jima told me she "knew a woman who had lost her husband at Iwo Jima" and arranged for me to meet with Mitsue. They were both Christians and attended the same church, where they had become friends despite the gap in their ages.

When I actually met Mitsue I saw that she was very much the kind of person to strike up a friendship with someone young enough to be her granddaughter. Sharp and funny, she was so full of life that she didn't seem like a nonagenarian. Her memory was excellent, and she told me everything about her husband—from his unexpected call-up to her getting news of his death—as if it had all happened yesterday.

I could hear the sound of the sea in the living room where I sat listening to Mitsue. It was only a two-minute walk from her house down to the beach where the waves of the Inland Sea lapped gently on the shore.

On May 21, 1946, Mitsue had flung an unvarnished box into this sea—a box of the kind designed to contain the ashes of the dead.

"When I got the announcement of his death, it said I should go and collect his remains. So I went to the government office, paid 100 yen, and was handed a plain wooden box in return. But when I looked inside, there were no remains at all, just a wooden Buddhist mortuary tablet with the words: 'Army Lieutenant Egawa Masaharu. Died in battle on Iwo Jima.' The cold-bloodedness of it made me so furious that on my way home I thought, 'Damn this thing,' and threw it into the sea."

All Mitsue was carrying when she got back home was the Buddhist mortuary tablet. She could not bring herself to throw away something that had her husband's name on it.

EGAWA MASAHARU WAS CALLED up on June 26, 1944. The Americans had already invaded Saipan by this time.

Masaharu had spent eight years in the United States, at the American branch of the Japanese bank for which he worked, before getting married, and he had many American friends. He was immune to wartime hysteria. Mitsue remembers him saying under his breath, "I don't want to fight a war that we're sure to lose," before adding, as if on second thought, "But I'm a smart fellow. I'm sure I'll make it back alive."

All the letters he sent from Iwo Jima were written on postcards—twenty-eight of them in total, of which thirteen were to his children.

Hello there, everybody. Are you all well? Daddy is working hard at being a soldier.

There are lots of little birds here called white-eyes. They're little birds that look like bush warblers, but the edges of their eyes are white. That's why they're called white-eyes.

Quite a long time ago, one of the soldiers caught a newborn white-eye. He put it in a cage and hung the cage from a low branch on a tree.

Every day, morning, noon, and night, the mother bird brings tasty food to feed it. The baby got bigger very fast and is learning to sing like its mother.

I want all three of you to always do what your mother tells you, and, just like the little baby white-eye, grow up to be good little children.

Your soldier daddy

There were many white-eyes on the island and the soldiers found their singing comforting. The birds had no fear of humans and would come right up to them, an indication of just how peaceful a place Iwo Jima had been until then.

Egawa's letter reminded me of some letters Kuribayashi had written to his youngest daughter, Takako. These also talked about young birds, though Kuribayashi was talking about chicks rather than white-eyes, as he was raising chickens for eggs as part of his effort to improve the food situation. On November 26, 1944, he wrote:

Tako-chan! One of Daddy's mommy-hens hatched four chicks today. One of the soldiers on guard duty got her to sit on seven eggs about twenty days ago. Today four chicks popped out and are crying cheep-cheep-cheep. There are ten other chickens who spend all their time catching insects to eat so they've become very big.

And on December 23, 1944, he wrote:

> *Tako-chan . . . the four chicks are very well indeed and play every day as they follow their mother around. They're always catching insects to eat. About three days after they were born, they started having fights.*

Kuribayashi mentions these four chicks for the third time in the last letter he wrote to Takako—on January 28, 1945. Both he and Egawa must have transferred memories of their wives and children at home onto the heartwarming sight of mother birds with their young: "The four chicks that were born two months ago have become very big. Every day they are led around by their mother to find things to eat. I'm sorry to say they are wrecking the field I went to so much trouble to plant!"

Not wanting to worry their little children, neither Egawa nor Kuribayashi mentioned the grim state of things on the island, but looked instead for enjoyable or unusual things to write about. Other fathers probably did the same.

Censorship, which restricted the subjects that could be discussed, may have played a part, but by itself it is not an adequate explanation. Surely discovering and describing charming and beautiful things was something they needed to do to help them get through the days at the front.

In a letter to his wife, Egawa wrote:

> *When my unit has morning roll-call, I chant them the Imperial instructions one by one in the calm and clear morning breeze. Then I make them perform the ceremony of distant worship and greetings to the Imperial Palace.*
>
> *Every evening, I assemble them for roll call with the beautiful southern sky and the palm trees in the background. After I have given them time to reflect carefully on the five clauses they swore to*

in the morning, as platoon commander I lead them in singing "Umi Yukaba" ["If I Go Away to Sea"]. The doctors tell me that the soldiers who are in the nearby sickroom can hear us faintly and it helps put them in a calm mood.

The forty-four-year-old Egawa was clearly performing the unfamiliar duties of a platoon leader with great diligence. Totally unlike his work as a banker, it was his first experience of military life in twenty years. It must have been tough, both physically and mentally.

The calm, clear morning breeze, the beautiful southern sky and the palms, the chorus of "Umi Yukaba" echoing faintly in the sickroom— we can see how Egawa was trying to clutch at any beauty he could find in the people or the nature around him out there on the brutal front.

There wasn't much to delight the eye or soothe the heart. Conscious of the situation her husband was in, Mitsue sent Egawa not only photographs of the children, but frequently sent pictures they had drawn and compositions they had written. Egawa would send back his opinions on a daily basis.

Your letters were all very well written. I think I understand your drawing, Nobuko [his four-year-old second daughter]. *Hiroko* [his six-year-old eldest daughter], *your pictures of a battledore and shuttlecock and the Japanese lantern are very well done. And I see you've not forgotten how to draw rabbits either.*

Jun [his eight-year-old son], *that steam train of yours is really something. It gave me a surprise. It's definitely the best train you've ever drawn.*

It was memories of his life as a father and husband back in Osaka that gave Egawa the strength he needed for life on the front. As he wrote to his wife:

*When evening comes and I can relax, I always enjoy myself
imagining the children, who'd be starving by this time, eating away
with great energy. I imagine myself sitting opposite from Nobuko
and even get the urge to speak to her.*

*The Japanese characters look better drawn every time you send
me something written by Jun and Hiroko. I supposed I'm a besotted
dad, but I feel happier somehow just holding them in my hand.*

There was not much time left for Egawa to console himself by looking at his children's pictures and handwriting. Eight days after the mail
service was canceled, the Americans invaded and the brutal battle began.

Mitsue will never know when, where, or how her husband died. The
battalion to which Egawa belonged was completely wiped out.

HE WAS THIRTY-SIX and she twenty-five when they got married.

Egawa had just returned to Japan from his eight-year stint in
America. A fan of Hani Motoko, who founded the liberal Jiyû Gakuen
private school and set up the pioneering women's magazine *Fujin no
Tomo* (*Woman's Friend*), Mitsue was working as a leader in Tomo no
Kai, an organization Hani had established to improve the quality of
everyday life.

They married late, according to the standards of the time. "We used
to laugh about my being 'a late goer' and him being 'a late receiver,' "
recalled Mitsue fondly.

They never once argued. When I asked her what sort of man her
husband was, she replied: "He was a good person. Everybody spoke
well of him. He was special: clever, kind, wasted on someone like me!
And he was tall and handsome, too."

On the day Egawa left for the front, Mitsue could not bear to listen
to the members of the neighborhood association cheering "banzai."

She thanked them and, slamming the door behind her, rushed back into the house and burst into tears.

Her husband no longer belonged to the family; he was a soldier working for the good of his country. She felt empty inside as she heard the footsteps of the crowd going to see him off at the station and the whistle of the train that was taking him away.

There was a notebook squeezed in between the pages of the scrapbook Mitsue had lent me. I looked inside. It contained line after line of neat writing in fountain pen. After the war, Mitsue had copied all the letters she had been sent by her husband.

"I thought I'd get the children to read them when they were a little bit older. See, the characters on the postcards are so small they're difficult to read."

It was true. Every square centimeter of the postcards was covered in little ideograms, and Egawa also had the kind of flowing, elegant hand that is difficult for children to read.

It turned out that there were actually two notebooks in the scrapbook, and the postcards had been faithfully copied into the second one, too. Mitsue had performed the same task twice.

Why two notebooks? I wanted to ask her, but I restrained myself. After the war, Mitsue had worked her fingers to the bone while also looking after her three children, an aging father-in-law, and a handicapped brother-in-law.

In my mind's eye I could picture her concentrating on copying her husband's letters long after the rest of the family had gone to bed. Meditating on the words her husband left behind and storing them in her heart must have somehow made the days easier to bear.

> *I am a commonplace, difficult husband, but as a wife you have really helped and supported me. As for the children, you are a good and diligent mother, and at this late stage I cannot properly express the gratitude I owe you.*

He thanks his wife formally like this and then continues:

> *There were many occasions when I should have expressed my*
> *gratitude to you—I had the means to do so after all—but I thought*
> *that the feeling of gratitude within me was enough by itself, so I did*
> *not make the effort to say "Thank you." It is something I regret*
> *deeply. Do not think badly of me. I hope you will forgive me.*

When he left for the front, Egawa told Mitsue he was sure he'd "make it back alive," but it is clear that he meant this letter to be his final message.

Fully aware that he was going to die, he ends his letter with the words: "Fight the good fight!" And Mitsue proved herself worthy of the trust her husband had placed in her. For sixty years after the war ended, she lived on, "fighting the good fight," just like all the other women who lost their husbands in that war.

A FEW DAYS AFTER meeting Egawa Mitsue, I came across the final message of a young soldier who had been on Iwo Jima; it had been published in the bulletin of the Association of Iwo Jima.

Egawa and Kuribayashi both wrote letters that were implicit "final messages" to their families, but this one actually bore the title "Final Message" at the head of the page. Written on unlined white paper, the characters neatly aligned and the brushwork perfect, it looked the way one feels a final message ought to look. I felt myself drawn to it—the stylized characters like those in a calligraphy textbook, and the youthful determination it exuded, so different from anything Kuribayashi or Egawa wrote.

The Association of Iwo Jima receives numerous inquiries about the personal effects of dead Japanese soldiers that American soldiers took back home with them from Iwo Jima. These might be army-issued notebooks, diaries, Rising Sun flags with good-luck messages written on them, or family photographs. Many such personal effects have been returned to the families of the dead.

This final message appeared in March 2004 in the "Does Anybody Know Anything About This?" section of the association's bulletin. A photocopy of the final message had been sent to the association in September of the year before.

Final Message

As one who was given life in order to serve the emperor, I was always ready for my corpse to lie in the field of battle. It is my long-cherished desire as a soldier.

I go to my death happily and with a feeling of calm. But the shame of being unable to perform my duty satisfactorily is unendurable.

My honorable father and mother, for more than twenty years I have caused you great bother; under your warm guardianship you raised me to be a fine man over five shaku *in height, and it is truly inexcusable that I am unable now to do anything for you in return. All I can do is express my warmest thanks.*

The young man goes on to say that he wants his 200 yen's worth of savings to be spent "for the country," tells them how his personal effects should be dealt with, sends his regards to his relatives and neighbors, and prays that his native village will thrive. He writes about how things were when he left for the front, which suggests that he did not compose the message in advance, but after getting to Iwo Jima.

In conclusion, I would like to wish good health and long life to you, Father and Mother, and to my big brothers and sisters Torao,

Kei, Eizô, Tadashi, Otaka, Suehara, and to Tatsumi, Fumiko,
and Tatsuko. Father and Mother, you are old now, so please take
care of yourselves.

My only regret is that I was never able to see the splendid new
house that you both worked so hard to build, Father and Mother. I
am sorry about that. For the rest, I have no regrets.

What was the young soldier thinking as he wrote the names of all
the members of his family? The first half of his final message is typically soldierly and stiff, but the part that follows the names of his six
older and three younger siblings shows some of the uncertainty one
would expect from a young man in his twenties.

By the time the soldier wrote this message there were probably no
more planes to deliver it to his family. Did he have his final message on
him as he fought in the battle? Even after his body rotted away, his final
message did not molder away into the earth of Iwo Jima but reaches out
across six decades.

No relative has stepped forward to claim it. Still undelivered, his
final message ends like this:

There is more that I would like to write, but I am so overwhelmed
by emotion that I cannot remember what it was.

> *Best Wishes.*
> *Tatsuo*
> *To my father and mother*

CHAPTER NINE

THE BATTLE

—

THE AMERICANS GAVE MOUNT SURIBACHI THE CODE NAME "HOT Rocks." Suribachi was a dormant volcano that only spat out the odd lick of steam here and there; nonetheless, quite a few marines were worried that the tremendous bombardment they were subjecting it to could reawaken it and provoke a volcanic eruption.

It was 10:31 a.m. on D-day plus four (February 23) that the Stars and Stripes first flew from the summit of Hot Rocks. The flag was a little on the small side—just 70 centimeters high by 135 centimeters wide—but the island was small enough that nearly all the marines there could see it. In their joy at having captured the mountain that symbolized the island, some cheered, some wept, and others waved their helmets in the air and whistled. The ships out at sea all sounded their horns together.

The wild enthusiasm of the American forces was in proportion to the massive damage they had suffered in the days between the landing and that moment. After D-day, which produced more casualties than they had expected, they had occupied Chidori Airfield and then divided the jobs of taking Mount Suribachi and the main Japanese defensive position northeast of the island. The Japanese continued to offer stiff resistance and the Americans were able to advance only from 50 to 500 meters a day. Many of the frontline officers were killed in action, and it was only on D-day plus three that the Americans were finally able to concentrate on taking Mount Suribachi, though it had seemed to be right there in front of them on the beach where they had landed.

The photograph of the six soldiers raising the flag that was featured on the front pages of newspapers and went on to be turned into a stamp and a bronze statue was not taken at this time, because the flag was actually raised on the summit of Suribachi on two separate occasions.

Immediately after the first flag had been raised, someone wanted to save it for a souvenir. That someone was Lieutenant Colonel Chandler W. Johnson, commanding officer of the Fifth Division, 28th Regiment, Second Battalion, to which the marines who went up the summit of Suribachi belonged. As they were about to start their ascent, Johnson handed one of them a flag he had brought ashore, "If you get to the top, put it up." He was thus the originator of the whole episode.

Johnson wanted to keep the first historic flag safe and raise a substitute in its place. And anyway, wouldn't a bigger flag be better? He therefore tracked down a second flag and had that taken up to the summit. The new flag measured 140 centimeters by 245 centimeters.

In this way, the first flag was taken down and a second flag was hoisted in its place. The celebrated photograph by Joe Rosenthal, an AP photographer, captured this second flag raising. His photograph not only reached Guam faster than the pictures of the first flag raising taken by the marine press corps, but had such magnificent composition and lighting that it ended up being featured in hundreds of newspapers.

Everything about the photograph—from the distribution of the soldiers to the way the flag was waving—was so perfect that a rumor circulated that the photographer had staged the whole thing. The truth was that Rosenthal had gotten there late and, barely in time for the second hoisting, had clicked the shutter in considerable haste.

Many Japanese people have seen this historic photograph; few, however, know what was used for the flagpole.

Lieutenant Colonel Johnson had given a flag to his men as they headed up Mount Suribachi, but he did not provide any flagpole for it. In both the first and second flag raisings, marines procured the poles from whatever was on the top of the mountain. It was Corporal Robert Leader and Private First Class Leo J. Rozek who found something that fit the bill: a length of metal piping that lay amid all the debris on the summit.

The pipe belonged to a cistern that the Japanese forces had built to collect rainwater for drinking. The cistern had been completely destroyed in the American air raids, and the pipe itself was riddled with holes.

To the marines, that pipe was no more than a piece of junk among a pile of debris. To the Japanese it was much more. The true value of that grubby pipe could only be understood by people who had known the agony of being parched, or had watched their comrades die begging for a drink of water.

The American soldiers had supplies of canned water to drink. During the battle, a Japanese soldier wrote in his diary: "I heard rumors that the Americans drink canned water. Is it possible such a thing exists in this world?" Of course it existed. Every landing craft was loaded with six thousand cans, each of which held eighteen liters of water—and there were seventy-three landing craft in all. The marines called Iwo Jima "hell," but at least they did not have to suffer from thirst.

The Stars and Stripes waved over Iwo Jima, a declaration of America's victory and America's conquest. But the pole that held that flag aloft was the wreckage of a system that had helped sustain life for the more than twenty thousand Japanese troops on the island. Frozen forever in that incomparable photograph, a cruel and bizarre juxtaposition is still exposed to the eyes of the world.

———

IMMEDIATELY AFTER THE FIRST flag had been raised on Mount Suribachi, a motorboat dropped off a number of men on the island. They disembarked on the stretch of shore that the Americans had dubbed "Green Beach," the corner of the south shore closest to the base of Mount Suribachi.

Two men stood side by side upon the black sand that four days before had clutched at the ankles of the marines and hampered the caterpillar tracks of the tanks. They had a good view of the Stars and Stripes fluttering on the summit of Mount Suribachi.

One of the men wore a gray sweatshirt over his khaki uniform. He said to his companion: "Holland, the raising of that flag means a Marine Corps for another five hundred years."

Holland was Lieutenant General Holland M. Smith. And the old general's eyes swam with tears as he thought back on all the heroic feats of "his marines" and all the casualties they had endured. This would be his last command.

The man in the sweatshirt was James V. Forrestal, secretary of the navy. Forrestal had come all the way out to the Pacific to witness firsthand the marine invasion of Iwo Jima and had been in the command ship USS *Eldorado* off the island, watching the campaign unfold.

Overriding the opposition of his entourage, who feared for his safety, he went ashore. Secretary Forrestal had walked the beaches of Normandy seven months earlier and was equally determined to inspect the Iwo Jima beachhead himself.

LIEUTENANT GENERAL SMITH was commanding general of the U.S. Marines Expeditionary Troops. The chain of command was as follows: above Smith stood Vice Admiral Richmond K. Turner, U.S. Navy, commander of the Joint Expeditionary Force; above Turner was Rear Admiral Raymond A. Spruance, commander of the Fifth Fleet; above him was Admiral Nimitz, commander in chief of the Pacific Fleet. Above them all was Navy Secretary Forrestal, who stood at the apex of the navy power structure.

Well aware that he could not allow the navy secretary to go ashore by himself, Lieutenant General Smith accompanied him and his entourage to the beach, and was thus able to witness a moment of history.

There was a rationale behind Forrestal's remark to Smith about "a Marine Corps for another five hundred years." The marines were often seen as little more than an afterthought or add-on to the navy. The question of whether there was a genuine need for them was often debated.

The Marine Corps was originally organized as an affiliate of the navy and was a small force responsible for onboard security and sharpshooting. Its role was reevaluated in the years after World War I. Suspecting that the islands of the Pacific could become the scene of fighting in the near future, the American military decided that an elite force specializing in amphibious landings was needed and gave that role to the marines. The American forces were running combat simulations against Japan in the Pacific years before Pearl Harbor, at a time when the Japanese military had not even started developing a strategy toward America.

Over time, the marines were built up as a force able to conduct independent amphibious operations far away from the continental United States. As the U.S. military establishment had predicted, the day came when battles had to be fought on the islands of the Pacific, and the marines acquitted themselves nobly in landing operations against the Japanese on Guadalcanal, Tarawa, Peleliu, Saipan, and Guam, among other places.

The Americans raising the Stars and Stripes on Iwo Jima—on the

Japanese homeland—was a historic moment. And it was the marines who did it. In so doing, they forcefully justified their existence and proclaimed their worth to the world.

The marines were the ones who landed under enemy fire and secured positions for the rear guard units to take up; the marines were the ones who first made contact with the enemy. But despite exposing themselves to greater danger in this manner, not only were they less respected than the other three services—the army, navy, and air force—they were also often looked down on as a bunch of ruffians. Now a single flag guaranteed that they would get the respect that their dangerous, brutal missions deserved for five hundred years—such was Secretary Forrestal's promise.

The following day, February 24, Forrestal left for Guam. With the landing operation completed and Mount Suribachi, seen as the island's key strategic point, in American hands, Forrestal thought he had seen everything he needed to see. But the fight was by no means over.

Neither the navy secretary nor the American public going crazy over the flag-raising photograph had any way of knowing that the marines would need another thirty days to conquer Iwo Jima completely.

Of the forty men who stood on the summit of Mount Suribachi at that historic moment, only four were able to walk on board the ships that would take them home. Of the remaining thirty-six, the lucky ones left on stretchers; the unlucky ones died and were buried on the island.

THE FALL OF MOUNT Suribachi within only four days of the Americans landing was a severe blow to Kuribayashi.

He had planned for the decisive battle to be fought from the defensive positions that ran from the center to the northern part of the island, so he was ready to let Suribachi go at some point, but he had hoped that the garrison defending the summit would hold out for a minimum of ten days and keep the enemy pinned down.

Mount Suribachi fell earlier chiefly because the tunnels linking it to the Motoyama area in the center of the island had not been completed in time. The Japanese had built a total of 18 kilometers of tunnels by the time the Americans landed, but those between Mount Suribachi and Motoyama had not yet been joined. Mount Suribachi was cut off when the Americans occupied Chidorigahara, which lay between the two.

Had the tunnels between Mount Suribachi and Motoyama been ready, it would have been possible to travel back and forth between the two installations without having to emerge aboveground. The Japanese would have been able to stay in contact; more important, they would have also been able to move troops, weapons, and ammunition. Kuribayashi must have bitterly regretted the shortage of materials that hampered his tunnel-building program.

The Americans landed on the south beach, then, while one group advanced to the left to take Mount Suribachi, other units headed right, pushing up to the northeast. The Japanese forces ranged against them fought back from defenses they had built in three tiers: the first line of defense; the second line of defense; and then the honeycomb defense. They cleverly exploited the uneven ground and their underground positions to conceal their guns, while the artillerymen were also waiting for the enemy underground.

Motoyama Airfield, in the center of the island, was the prize the Americans most wanted to capture. The Japanese first and second lines of defense were placed on either side of this airfield, above and below it. The marines' Fourth and Fifth Divisions, which pushed toward Motoyama Airfield, encountered stiff resistance from the Japanese and suffered many casualties. This inspired the Americans to send in the reserved Third Division on February 24, the day after the capture of Mount Suribachi. The total manpower committed by the Americans now rose to around sixty-one thousand men—three full marine divisions—and for the next four days the battle in the area around Motoyama Airfield became very intense.

The Americans chose to make a frontal assault based on brute strength.

They advanced northward, tanks out in front and artillery units blasting round after round from their rocket guns. The infantry followed, using flamethrowers, hand grenades, and high explosives to wipe out the pillboxes and underground bunkers one by one. Rear Admiral Rinosuke Ichimaru summed up the situation in a *Senkun Denpô*— literally a "war lesson telegram"—he sent to the Imperial General Headquarters. "The Americans only advance after making a desert out of everything before them. Their infantry advance at a speed of about ten meters an hour. They fight with a mentality as though exterminating insects."

The Japanese forces fired from cleverly concealed gun ports, as well as raining down concentrated fire from mortars and rocket guns. When the firepower of the Americans became simply too overwhelming, they would slip down into their underground installations and go through one of the tunnels that headed off any which way, then resume the attack from some unexpected point. The different units could coordinate by keeping in contact via a telephone system that ran through the tunnels.

This was the style of fighting Kuribayashi had envisaged and prepared for over the previous eight months.

The underground bunkers and tunnels the soldiers had sweated so hard to construct gave them a standby location before making a sortie, and a place to take refuge from enemy gunfire. They also served as their living quarters, offering shelter from the airstrikes that went on throughout the battle, as well as providing storage space for food and ammunition. The soldiers must have recognized that this was the only way they could fight on such a small island against an enemy so superior in numbers, firepower, and equipment.

Admiral Nimitz acknowledged that Kuribayashi had turned Iwo Jima into "the most impregnable eight-square-mile island base in the

Pacific." "The only thing we could do," he stated, "was to use infantry units supported by tanks to get in and capture one by one the bases the Japanese had so ingeniously constructed."

The Japanese soldiers would also sprint out of their caves clutching armor-piercing charges (bombs capable of destroying the armor-plating of tanks) and blow up tanks by flinging themselves against them. These close-quarters attacks on tanks traditionally involved throwing explosive charges into the tank's caterpillar tracks and then withdrawing, but when it came to real combat many soldiers summoned up the courage to ram themselves bodily against the tanks, which was much more effective. It goes without saying that they were blown to pieces when the charge went off. They were doing on land what the Kamikaze Special Attack Force was doing in the air.

Summing up what was unique about the extraordinary close-quarters battle between underground and aboveground waged by Kuribayashi, Lieutenant General Smith declared in *Coral and Brass* that: "Every cave, every pillbox, every bunker was an individual battle, where Japanese and Marine fought hand to hand to the death."

The Japanese put up a desperate fight, but lost Motoyama Airfield by February 26, after the Americans sent in reinforcements and blanketed the area with devastating artillery barrages. By the evening of February 27, Japanese troop strength had been cut by half, while guns and ammunition had shrunk by two thirds. The ammunition situation for field guns and midsize trench mortars was especially dire, with only 10 percent of the original stock remaining.

The Japanese were now no longer able to respond in kind to American firepower. Henceforth they could not expect to fight in a manner that resembled any conventional idea of what a battle should be; from then on, the battle would be one of bloodshed and endurance more painful than death itself. Nor would Kuribayashi allow his men to use death as a quick way out.

"Yours not to die a noble and heroic death; yours to live the most excruciating life"——that was the role that Kuribayashi, commander in chief on this grimmest of battlegrounds, ordered his soldiers to perform.

ÔKOSHI HARUNORI WAS A Japanese soldier who was wounded on Iwo Jima and became a prisoner of war. He passed through prison camps in San Francisco, Chicago, and Hawaii before being repatriated in January 1947. As a navy special junior soldier, Ôkoshi was still only seventeen years old when he fought on Iwo Jima. He was among the youngest POWs in the camps, but when it came out that he was an "Iwo Jima soldier," the guards would always treat him slightly differently. Says Ôkoshi: "One of the American soldiers told me that 'Kamikaze soldiers' and 'Iwo Jima soldiers' were special."

Ishii Shûji, another prisoner of war, recalled an experience he had in the POW camp in San Francisco.

One day, one of the guards asked me: "So where were you captured?"

"Iwo Jima," I replied.

The guard started, went pale, and adjusted his grip on his weapon. That gave all of us quite a surprise, too.

In the camps, the Japanese soldiers who had been captured on Iwo Jima were regarded with a mixture of fear and respect. The Americans all knew how fiercely they had fought.

There was nothing special about the garrison that defended Iwo Jima in terms of age, physical strength, and combat experience. The marines were a combination of veteran officers and physically strong volunteers with high morale, but the Japanese forces included many conscripts. The only proper cohesive fighting units were the 145th Infantry Regiment and the 26th Tank Regiment; otherwise the garrison was made up of independent infantry and artillery battalions and auxiliary units.

But even while they expended huge amounts of physical energy in building defensive positions, the pace of training never slackened, so that the soldiers were able to improve their fighting skills. It was probably their desire to defend Iwo Jima, a part of Japan itself, and to stave off air raids and the invasion of the homeland that more than anything else transformed them into such a crack force.

Kuribayashi gave extremely practical directions regarding training. I will quote the "Battle Directions for the Soldiers of Courage Division" in its entirety. ("Courage" was a single Japanese ideogram that served as a sort of code name for the Division.) These directions were devised and distributed by Kuribayashi.

Preparations for battle

1. Use every moment you have, whether during air raids or during battle, to build strong positions that enable you to smash the enemy at a ratio of ten to one.
2. Build fortifications that enable you to shoot and attack in any direction without pausing even if your comrades should fall.
3. Be resolute and make rapid preparations to store food and water in your position so that your supplies will last even through intense barrages.

Fighting defensively

1. Destroy the American devils with heavy fire. Improve your aim and try to hit your target the first time.

2. As we practiced, refrain from reckless charges, but take advantage of the moment when you've smashed the enemy. Watch out for bullets from others of the enemy.

3. When one man dies a hole opens up in the defense. Exploit man-made structures and natural features for your own protection. Take care with camouflage and cover.

4. Destroy enemy tanks with explosives, and several enemy soldiers along with the tank. This is your best chance for meritorious deeds.

5. Do not be alarmed should tanks come toward you with a thunderous rumble. Shoot at them with antitank fire and use tanks.

6. Do not be afraid if the enemy penetrates inside your position. Resist stubbornly and shoot them dead.

7. Control is difficult to exercise if you are sparsely dispersed over a wide area. Always tell the officers in charge when you move forward.

8. Even if your commanding officer falls, continue defending your position, by yourself if necessary. Your most important duty is to perform brave deeds.

9. Do not think about eating and drinking, but focus on exterminating the enemy. Be brave, O warriors, even if rest and sleep are impossible.

10. The strength of each one of you is the cause of our victory. Soldiers of Courage Division, do not crack at the harshness of the battle and try to hasten your death.

11. We will finally prevail if you make the effort to kill just one man more. Die after killing ten men and yours is a glorious death on the battlefield.

12. Keep on fighting even if you are wounded in the battle. Do not get taken prisoner. At the end, stab the enemy as he stabs you.

It is this sort of thoroughgoing attention to detail that distinguishes Kuribayashi as a commander.

The document contains neither vapid ideals nor meaningless, flowery rhetoric. Kuribayashi thought carefully about what was likely to unnerve his men and what mistakes they were likely to make, then told them in simple terms what they needed to be aware of in the heat of battle.

As soon as the real battle began, Kuribayashi started reviewing the achievements of the men under him. He then awarded letters of commendation (testimonials from the commander in chief) and requests for promotion based on these.

On February 19, the day the Americans landed, Second Lieutenant Nakamura Sadao, a platoon commander of the Eighth Independent Anti-Tank Battalion, immobilized twenty tanks. Kuribayashi quickly awarded him a personal letter of commendation and petitioned for a double promotion of rank. Sadao's achievement even attained *jōbun*, meaning that his feat was reported to the emperor, a quite exceptional honor at the time.

Kuribayashi continued to review the exploits of his soldiers carefully, awarding them letters of commendation or arranging for their deeds to be reported to the emperor. The offical history records that Kuribayashi issued four letters of commendation, all of which were relayed to the emperor in *jōbun*. This sort of painstaking scrupulosity was not displayed by the other commanding officers in the Pacific War theater. Presumably Kuribayashi was making some sort of effort to reward his men for their achievements. The responsible officer from the adjutant division directly under Kuribayashi would make his perilous way through the thick of the fighting to deliver the testimonials to the different units.

These letters of commendation were also sent to the Imperial Headquarters and preserved in the official records. On Iwo Jima few survived and most records of the battle were lost, so the testimonials, which record who did what and where, provide insights into how the battle unfolded.

Since the testimonials were preserved in the official record, they were also communicated to the soldiers' families. This was not only a matter of pride for the whole family, but knowing how their husbands, fathers, and sons had acquitted themselves in combat must have been some consolation for the bereaved families.

Of course, the soldiers who were awarded letters of commendation were not alone in fighting bravely. When communications were cut and reports could no longer be transmitted or when entire units were wiped out, inevitably nothing made it to the record. No doubt many exploits deserving letters of commendation went unrewarded.

In a sense, the battle on Iwo Jima was about more than acts of heroism. There were wounded soldiers who weakened and died for lack of medical care; soldiers who suffocated when their bunkers were blasted shut; soldiers who burned to death when gasoline was poured into the bunkers and ignited. And there were others who never returned when they ran through the hail of bullets to deliver messages or fetch water for their comrades.

Death in battle is always cruel. But if death in battle is death with honor, then every sort of death—including the deaths of those who died trembling and afraid, or bitterly wishing they could be back at home—should be classified as "death with honor."

The Japanese soldiers believed that, as long as they stayed alive and continued with their resistance, Iwo Jima would not fall. So they lived in agony and they died in agony. On Iwo Jima, every facet of living and of dying was part of the battle.

Kuribayashi was concerned about the families of his men. Major Komoto Kumeji, a senior adjutant, was away in Tokyo liaising with the Imperial General Headquarters when the Americans invaded the island, and thus found himself unable to return. He received a message from Kuribayashi at the end of February while the battle was still raging. It said: "Adjutant Komoto, I want you to deal with the posthumous affairs of the soldiers on Iwo Jima with the utmost thoroughness." Kuribayashi knew he would not be able to send his men back home alive, but as this brief order shows, he was determined that at the very least Senior Adjutant Komoto should help their families.

In response to Kuribayashi's wish, Komoto established the Iwo Jima Survey Group together with a number of soldiers below officer class from units on Iwo Jima who were in Tokyo performing such duties as escorting home the bones of the dead. The Group devoted itself to preparing and dispatching bulletins listing the men who had died in action and recording acts of heroism. Their activities continued to the end of 1945, beyond the end of the war.

BY THE BEGINNING of March two thirds of the island was in American hands. They had broken through both the first defense line and the second defense line and had captured all the airfields, including the northernmost of the three, Kita Airfield. The Japanese forces were being boxed into the island's northernmost tip.

By D-day plus thirteen (March 4), the surviving manpower of the Japanese amounted to some forty-one hundred men. Two thirds of the Japanese officers had been killed, and the bulk of their artillery and tanks were lost.

This was the day when an American plane landed on Chidori Airfield for the first time. A B-29 based in Saipan, it had taken part in a bombing run on Tokyo but was forced to make an emergency landing on the home leg due to mechanical failure and lack of fuel. Although Japanese mortar fire forced it to take off again quickly, the landing was a sign that the capture of Iwo Jima was starting to deliver concrete results for the American side.

In contrast, the Japanese, running out of ammunition, started switching to guerrilla tactics.

The Americans pushed forward steadily. The Japanese did not retreat but defended their positions to the death. Inevitably the battle turned into close-quarters combat, with both sides close enough to make out each other's faces. The Americans could not provide air support for fear of harming their own side, so they pushed forward with flamethrowers and satchel charges. The Japanese responded by throwing grenades from their subterranean bunkers or sniping with small arms.

As the supply of explosives started to run out, the Japanese were no longer able to destroy enemy tanks in suicide attacks. I saw a photograph where a can of gasoline thought to have been stolen from the Americans lay near the corpses of three Japanese soldiers who had thrown themselves against a tank. It is thought that they made their charge clutching the fuel can in lieu of explosives. One of the soldiers lies on his back. His stomach has been half blown away, but his arms, burned black, are thrust up into the air as if the can were still clasped in his hands.

The Japanese also conducted surprise attacks on the American camps at night. These were not banzai charges, but well-planned operations conducted by small numbers of men. Initially they were effective, but in time the Americans devised countermeasures, and few of the attackers made it back alive.

The underground bunkers echoed with the groans of the wounded and were suffused with the smell of sulfur and the stench of death. The Japanese had no way of burying the men who died in the bunkers and were forced to share their living space with their dead comrades.

Little in the way of food was left, but most excruciating of all was the lack of water. Even when the Japanese were digging the bunkers, before the American invasion, the lack of water had been hard enough to bear, but there had at least been a fixed ration of water, albeit a modest one. Without exception, the oral and written testimonies of survivors all talk about the suffering caused by the shortage of water at this stage.

Hoshino Fujitaka, formerly of the 20th Independent Artillery Mortar Battalion, recalled this time in a letter he sent to the bulletin of the Association of Iwo Jima: "I don't think I will ever be able to forget the memory of how sweet the rainwater that formed puddles in the tunnels in the night tasted when we got down on all fours to drink it." There is an old Japanese saying: "Sip on muddy water if you want to stay alive," but on Iwo Jima even muddy water was felt to be a blessing equal to the sweetest nectar.

Kojima Takatsugi, a survivor from the same battalion, published a memoir in the *Yanai Nichinichi Shimbun* newspaper in 1968. It contains the following passage:

As we waited for the Grummans to pull out, we used to gather in the entrance to the bunker and talk endlessly about the good old days back home. Our main topics were eating and water. Our battalion was made up of men from Korea [the 20th Independent Artillery Mortar Battalion was composed of Japanese people living in Korea], so we could temporarily slake our thirst by talking about how we'd like to drink a bellyful of the water of Hankou, or discussing things that had to do with water like the Tedong River and the Sambang waterfall.

One soldier suddenly shouted out for us all to come and see. We were thrilled to see that there was dew glistening on the tips of the Japanese pampas grass that was still in the shade. We pressed it to our lips as if in a silent kiss.

In this far from expertly written passage, the phrase "We pressed it to our lips as if in a silent kiss" stands out for its poetic beauty. That is how desperate they were for water. That is how precious fresh water was to them.

The memoir continues:

> One soldier got dreadfully down and started whimpering some sort of prayer: if his life—which looked likely to be snuffed out any day—was saved, and by some miracle he was able to return home safely, then he did not need status or fame. If he had to climb up into the clouds, then he would climb up into the clouds; if he had to walk on the seafloor, then he'd do that, too; but more than anything he wanted to get out of this hell on earth, he said.

"Hell on earth"—it wasn't just the common soldiers who felt that way, as this passage, transmitted to Imperial General Headquarters on March 5 by the chief of staff of the "Courage Division," makes clear.

> The air supremacy of the enemy is absolute and total, sometimes reaching a total of 1,600 planes in a single day. The truth is that from before dawn until nightfall, without even a moment's pause, they have from twenty or thirty to one hundred or more fighters in the air, strafing us and bombing us relentlessly. The enemy do not just put a halt to our daytime combat activities this way, but the support enables them to safely come up close, protected by tanks, and insolently penetrate those points where we are short of men.
>
> On our side, we are almost unable to respond as our artillery and heavy armaments have all been destroyed. In the present situation, all we can do is engage the enemy—who is always our superior in terms of material—with small arms and with hand grenades in a succession of difficult battles.
>
> *My battle report ends here. And from this living hell which com-*

pletely surpasses imagination, I take the liberty of sending in my re-
port as it is, although it may appear that I am merely whining. [Emphasis in the original.]

It is unusual to describe battle conditions as a "living hell" in a "war-lesson telegram," but by this time there was no one left alive on Iwo Jima who did not think of the place as hell. Reading the last emphasized sentence you seem to hear all the surviving soldiers crying out to you.

The chief of staff may have been the one who sent this message, but as commander in chief Kuribayashi approved all the telegrams transmitted from Iwo Jima. Extreme though the text of this particular telegram may be, it nonetheless expresses Kuribayashi's personal intent. He tried to give the Imperial General Headquarters a taste of what things were really like on the island they had written off, the island they had ordered him to defend to the end at a cost of more than twenty thousand Japanese lives.

To never complain. To never indulge in self-pity. To take whatever was thrown at you and to die in stoic silence. That was the proper conduct for a military man of the time. But Kuribayashi did not want to play by those rules.

KURIBAYASHI PROVIDED FAITHFUL REPORTS of the shifting tides of battle in his war-lesson telegrams. The Japanese expected that Americans would invade Taiwan and Okinawa after Iwo Jima. In an effort to help with their defense, Kuribayashi tried his best to form an accurate idea of enemy numbers while offering observations and analysis of the Americans' strategy and tactics.

A comparison of Kuribayashi's reports with the American military records published after the war shows that he had an accurate grasp of the damage the Americans had sustained. On March 2, for example,

Kuribayashi estimated American casualties at around twelve thousand, with about two hundred tanks and about sixty planes lost. His estimates are only around 10 percent above the correct figures.

Throughout the Pacific War, the Japanese commanders had a tendency to interpret the war in a way that was flattering for them. Kuribayashi was different: he was able to face the facts, calmly and head-on.

Kuribayashi sent his last war-lesson telegram on March 7. The longest telegram to be sent from Iwo Jima, it is unique in two respects.

First, it is addressed to Hasunuma Shigeru, chief aide-de-camp to the emperor. Hasunuma had been a professor of military science when Kuribayashi was at the Army War College, and was also a fellow cavalryman.

War-lesson telegrams were always addressed to the chief of staff at Imperial General Headquarters because they were considered useful input for subsequent strategic planning and battle directives. Addressing one to the chief aide-de-camp of the emperor was thus a case of "getting the wrong man," something that would never occur under normal circumstances.

Just like any other "war-lesson telegram," this telegram purports to be addressed to the vice chief of staff, but there is a note at its head that reads: "This telegram should be communicated to Hasunuma, chief aide-de-camp to the Emperor." The text, too, is directed at Hasunuma personally. "With the end of my life before me, I express my heartfelt thanks for your many years of kindness, and I pray that Your Honor will enjoy good fortune in war for a long time," says the last sentence—the whole thing reads like a final message to Hasunuma.

Why should Kuribayashi do this? The answer to that question lies in the second atypical feature of this war-lesson telegram. This second anomaly is the war lesson itself. In his analysis of the battle, Kuribayashi is overtly critical of the policies of the Imperial General Headquarters.

There are two points to the critique. First, it says that headquarters personnel were not wholeheartedly committed to the policy of inland defense and "endurance engagement with heavy bloodshed," but remained attached to the old doctrine of defense at the water's edge.

The Imperial General Headquarters had switched to a policy of inland defense in August 1944. On Iwo Jima, this did not translate into committing 100 percent of resources into their inland defenses, as the garrison was also ordered to build defensive positions at the water's edge. The navy was particularly stubborn in its insistence on constructing positions on the shore.

Although the military command realized from what had happened in Saipan that it was impossible to destroy the enemy at the water's edge, they were still incapable of making a bold policy U-turn. They retained a vestigial belief in shoreline defensive positions, with the result that Iwo Jima's defenses were neither one thing nor the other.

"Given the enemy's supremacy at sea and in the air, it was impossible for us to prevent them from landing. We should therefore not have been unduly concerned about their landing per se, but should have focused on our inland defenses and making dispositions accordingly," says the message. "We needed to prepare the key strong points of the main defenses thoroughly. The reason we could not do that was that much material, manpower, and time were squandered on the water's edge defenses I mentioned above." The most serious problem is that the main defenses remained uncompleted because of a policy that did not focus fully on either goal.

The second criticism was that the men were made to work on expanding the airfield until immediately prior to the American landing, despite no longer having airplanes. The telegram says: "Due to orders from the navy central command, manpower was diverted for the expansion of No. 1 and No. 2 airfields right up to the point when it was

204 | KUMIKO KAKEHASHI

clear that the enemy intended to invade, and this despite the fact that we had no planes. Our defenses thus grew weaker and weaker, which is deplorable."

Iwo Jima was originally conceived of as an unsinkable aircraft carrier out at sea. In accord with that, the original number-one priority had been to maintain and enlarge its airfields. But it flew in the face of logic not just to retain that policy, but to actually divert manpower for airfield expansion when it was almost certain that the Americans would invade and the most important challenge was to help the island hold out as long as possible. To top it all off, they had almost no usable airplanes, and ultimately the airfield the Japanese worked so hard to expand ended up being used by the Americans to conduct air raids on the Japanese homeland.

These two problems—the lack of thoroughness in implementing inland defense and the stubborn focus on the airfields—were both the result of the navy sticking to its original policies. Kuribayashi was an army lieutenant general, but he was also the commander in chief of Iwo Jima, meaning that the navy came under his authority. The navy, however, had its own way of doing things, and this prevented Kuribayashi's policies from being fully implemented.

There was antagonism between the navy and the army on Iwo Jima while the defenses were being built, and it persisted until the American landing. For Kuribayashi, the cause of this was the central commands of army and navy being at odds with each other, something that stopped them from having a consistent and integrated defense strategy for the island. As he points out in the war-lesson telegram: "The crucial thing is to get rid of the tendency of the army and navy to be territorial, and for both parties to become unified."

This war-lesson telegram is recorded in the official history, but the part that criticizes the army and navy for their territoriality and urges them to unite is omitted. The National Institute of Defense Studies compiled the official history, but it seems that the rivalry between the army and the navy was a taboo they wanted to steer well clear of, even in the age of the postwar Self-Defense Force.

Kuribayashi must have known that a message like this stood a good chance of being ignored if addressed directly to the Imperial General Headquarters. That is why he resorted to sending it to a former professor whom he trusted implicitly.

How did Chief Aide-de-Camp Hasunuma act when he received it?

The Diary of Kido Kôichi (Marquis Kido Kôichi was Lord Keeper of the Privy Seal) contains the following entry for March 9, 1945: "At 12:30 the chief aide-de-camp [Hasunuma] came into the room and we spoke about unifying the high command and so forth." "Unifying the high command and so forth" is the matter of unifying the army and the navy—the very subject Kuribayashi broached in his war-lesson telegram.

The question of whether or not to unify the army and the navy was being debated in Japan at the time. There was nothing new about the problem of the two services not coordinating with each other or being at each other's throats, but with the final battle for the homeland looming, it was reemerging as a very serious issue.

On February 26, a top-level meeting of the Army Central Office determined the "Basic Principles for Successful Execution of the Final Battle for the Homeland," and made the unification of the army and the navy a key theme. Based on this document, negotiations were held between the army and the navy beginning March 3. It was right at this time that Chief Aide-de-Camp Hasunuma met Lord Keeper of the Privy Seal Kido to discuss this subject.

Kuribayashi sent his final war-lesson telegram from Iwo Jima at 11:00 p.m. on March 7. The Imperial General Headquarters received it and passed it on to the vice chief of staff at 7:15 a.m. on March 8. Since Chief Aide-de-Camp Hasunuma paid his visit to Lord Keeper of the Privy Seal Kido at 12:30 p.m. on March 9, he must have gone to meet him after having read Kuribayashi's telegram. Hasunuma obviously understood that Kuribayashi was trying to communicate what things were really like on the front lines.

Ultimately, the unification of the army and the navy never came to pass. Although the top brass of the two services held meetings, they were unable to find common ground, and on March 26, former war minister Sugiyama reported their conclusion to the emperor: the unification of the army and the navy was "difficult and problematic." Their lack of unity on thinking about strategy persisted until the end of the war.

The words that conclude Kuribayashi's final war-lesson telegram can be seen as a criticism of the whole reckless war: "Most fatal for our defense is the enormous material gap between the two sides that places such a gulf between us. Ultimately we simply do not have the capacity to successfully implement any tactics or countermeasures."

This "enormous material gap between the two sides" is the discrepancy in the industrial and military might of the two nations.

Out at the front there was a brilliant commander in chief and brave soldiers willing to sacrifice their lives ungrudgingly. But no matter how many of them died, it was not enough to bridge the gap in relative strength between the two countries that had been there from the start. When Kuribayashi says, "We simply do not have the capacity to successfully implement any tactics or countermeasures," my guess is that he was not talking only about Iwo Jima, but about the entire war.

The telegram was stern in its disdain for the war leaders who, after first rushing into war without assessing its realities, then produced no more than a series of makeshift policies to get them out of whatever their present difficulties happened to be. Using a war-lesson telegram as his mouthpiece, Kuribayashi was able to say things that the average soldier could not say even if he wanted to, and that the officers on the ground, who believed in the ethos of fighting and keeping their mouths shut, would never have dreamed of saying.

Before being sent to Iwo Jima, Kuribayashi was a sophisticated, rather bookish sort of soldier—not at all the type to let his emotions get the better of him and to openly defy his superiors. But the merciless brutality of the battle in which his twenty thousand men were embroiled probably drove him to voice his complaint. His final war-lesson telegram was simultaneously a well-argued critique and a desperate protest on behalf of the men who were dying around him.

Imperial General Headquarters added a warning in bold brush-strokes above the densely packed text of the telegram: "Handle with care." In the end, the lessons Kuribayashi had learned from fighting, and imparted in his telegram, were not allowed to influence the way the Japanese military conducted the war thereafter.

CHAPTER TEN

THE END

—

THE NIGHT OF MARCH 9 WAS CLEAR. A WARM SEA BREEZE BLEW across the island littered with shrapnel and the corpses of soldiers.

As the surviving Japanese soldiers took a brief rest from their labors or groaned from the pain of wounds, deep down in their subterranean bunkers, a formation of 334 B-29 Superfortress bombers, their enormous fuselages shining silver, flew by high overhead at 8,000 meters. They had taken off from Guam, Saipan, and Tinian; it took them three hours just to form up; and the formation now stretched 100 kilometers from one end to the other. Their course was north. Their destination, Tokyo.

The Japanese base on Iwo Jima that had previously detected incoming American bombers on its radar and alerted the mainland or scrambled fighters to intercept them was no longer functioning, and the huge B-29 formation reached Tokyo with almost no resistance from fighters or antiaircraft guns. It was the early hours of the morning of March 10.

A total of 1,665 tons of incendiary bombs were dropped from a low altitude of less than 3,000 meters. A strong wind spread the fire, and the flames engulfed Tokyo's old downtown.

Around 84,000 people—there are also estimates of 100,000—were killed; around 40,000 were injured; and around 267,000 homes were destroyed by fire, leaving more than a million people homeless.

What set the great air raids on Tokyo apart were the murderous fires caused by incendiaries.

The M69 incendiary bomb used in the raids had been developed through repeated testing with the specific aim of burning down Japanese wooden houses. The M69 would explode on impact only after passing through the roof of a house and spewing out a burning gel that turned the surrounding area into a sea of fire. Dropping these on an urban area meant killing ordinary civilians indiscriminately, and up until then the Americans had refrained from using them for humanitarian reasons.

But in January 1945, Henry Arnold, commanding general of the U.S. Army Air Forces, was advised that the method followed until then—targeted bombing of munitions factories—was proving ineffective, and he changed the commander of the base in the Marianas. General Hansell, who had practiced the pinpoint bombing of military facilities, was dismissed, to be replaced by Major General Curtis LeMay, who was a proponent of indiscriminate strategic bombing using incendiaries.

Even before things reached this point, Kuribayashi had already been worrying that incendiaries might be used to bomb Tokyo, setting off huge fires. He had repeatedly written to his family to warn them, as this November 2, 1944, letter to his wife, Yoshii, shows:

> . . . *In somewhere like Tokyo, the number of casualties it will cause is beyond imagining. Particularly if the enemy mixes in incendiary bombs, fires are sure to break out and cause immense confusion and catastrophe. You must be very, very resolute and make the proper preparations. The enemy has large planes close by and may well carry out raids on Tokyo.*

On December 15, 1944, he again warned Yoshii:

> *I know the mainland has recently started to be bombed frequently and I am very worried. It seems that for now they are targeting mili-*

tary factories, but we cannot know where they'll bomb indiscrimi-
nately. The fires that follow the bombing are still more difficult to
deal with, and you have to be on your guard all the time.

The dropping of incendiary bombs and the resulting fires, air
raids on Tokyo with large-size planes, the indiscriminate bombing of
places that were not military-related—Kuribayashi's forecasts all came
true.

The last letter he sent to his family was written on February 3. In it
Kuribayashi urges them to be on guard against air raids on Tokyo, particularly incendiary bombs:

> *As I always say, there's a good chance that the enemy air raids*
> *will multiply in intensity to many times their present level from*
> *spring onwards, so I think you should quickly go somewhere safe*
> *while you are still able to do so. It's unlikely you'll be killed by a*
> *bomb proper, but you must understand that there is a considerable*
> *danger of being killed by the fire caused by an incendiary.*
>
> *They have started dropping large numbers of incendiaries where*
> *I am and fires occur although there's nothing to burn here. (In addi-*
> *tion to normal incendiaries, they also drop drums of gasoline that*
> *turn everything into a veritable sea of fire—in Tokyo they may not*
> *be able to do that.)*

Kuribayashi's worries were on the mark—in the worst way possible.

IN *IWO JIMA*, Richard F. Newcomb, who served as a naval correspondent during World War II, describes the March 10 air raid on Tokyo as
"the most destructive raid of the war, in Europe or Japan, with horrors
beyond description." He continues: "The holocaust exceeded any con-
flagration in the Western World, including the burning of Rome by Nero

in 64 A.D., the London fire of 1666, the burning of Moscow in 1812, the Chicago fire of 1871, and the San Francisco earthquake of 1906."

The area destroyed by fire was around 40 square kilometers and covered Tokyo's Kôtô, Sumida, and Taitô wards. The leading squadrons dropped their incendiaries around the edges of the target area to create a wall of fire. After thus making it impossible for the residents to escape, the units that followed then bombed everything inside this ring— carpet-bombing, it was called.

With high-temperature gasoline gel burning, this was no ordinary fire. The flames would surge along the ground, then leap up into the sky like a tornado. According to testimony from the B-29 crews, the heat of the fire was so intense that it created turbulence that shook the planes violently as they flew at low altitude. There was no human means to extinguish the fire. The only thing people could do was run helplessly this way and that.

The furious flames sucked the oxygen out of the atmosphere and some people suffocated to death. People who had taken refuge in buildings made of reinforced concrete like schools, which were thought to be safe, were incinerated by the fire, which blew in with the power of a bomb blast. The rivers were choked with the corpses of people who had leaped in to escape from the inferno of scorching heat.

The night sky reflected the fire raging below and became as bright as day. The raid lasted two and a half hours, and when the crews of the B-29s looked back as they headed home, they could still see the sky above Tokyo glowing white from 300 kilometers away.

Two B-29s that had sustained damage in the Tokyo bombing landed on the runway of Iwo Jima on the way back. Another fourteen planes ditched into the sea nearby, and five of their crews were rescued.

The great air raid on Tokyo was on a colossal scale, but of the 334 B-29s that took part, only 14 planes failed to make it back safely. Iwo Jima contributed to this low rate of attrition. Ironically, it was the

Japanese who had originally built the runway that helped to save the Americans who had carried out the important task of burning Tokyo to the ground.

Just a few hundred meters north of that runway the Japanese soldiers were continuing with their painful resistance. They believed that they were having shells rained down on them in place of the citizens in the homeland. They believed that as long as they could hold out against the enemy, their fathers, mothers, wives, and children would all be safe—and the thought gave them hope.

Seven of the B-29s from the March 12 bombing raid on Nagoya, and thirteen of the B-29s on their way back from Kôbe on March 17 made emergency landings on Iwo Jima. Some of the crew members whose lives were saved this way got out of their planes, knelt down, and kissed the earth.

The American fighting men on the island were flabbergasted at the sight. As far as they were concerned, the island was hell itself: what could be crazier than kissing the floor of hell? But the B-29 crews were deeply thankful for the existence of this burned-up, ugly island that stood at the halfway point on the long haul back to their base in the Marianas.

Major General Curtis LeMay, the commander who had proposed and implemented the strategy of indiscriminate bombing with incendiaries, took part in the Kôbe raid as pilot of the lead plane. At a press conference in Saipan after the Kôbe raid, he declared: "Iwo Jima is really making the job easier."

In total, some 2,400 B-29s made emergency landings on Iwo Jima, saving the lives of around 27,000 crew members.

Iwo Jima was not used only for emergency landings. After the island had fallen completely, large numbers of fighters were needed to protect the B-29s, and then B-29s were stationed there. The Americans were now able to devastate any Japanese city at will. The raids on the mainland became fiercer, and the damage they inflicted ever more destructive. The air corridor to the homeland opened by the capture of Iwo Jima was a road that led to the final victory of the United States.

The number of lives saved by the island was higher than the number lost in the battle for it, and an air corridor that could speed up their victory had been secured. These two factors persuaded the American military that the historically unprecedented casualty levels incurred during the capture of Iwo Jima were worth it.

What was Kuribayashi doing on the night of March 10 when Tokyo was reduced to ashes?

He was burning bank notes in the Command Center. The notes were National Defense Contributions levied on his soldiers in the midst of the fierce fighting. There was a total of 36,584 yen. The surviving soldiers had handed over any money they had on them in the hope that it might help in the defense of the homeland.

There was simply no way to send the money back from an island as southerly and remote as Iwo Jima. So after the total had been tallied up, the bank notes, which the men had pulled out from ragged pockets or haversacks, soiled with soot and mud, were burned. Then a telegram was sent to the Imperial General Headquarters, asking them to contribute the equivalent sum to the Ministry of Finance. The telegram read: "My tears flow at the kindness of the men. Please do what is necessary to take care of the contribution that I had to burn tonight in this bunker."

Kuribayashi and his men had no way of knowing that an indiscriminate bombing raid on the capital city had been carried out that day as a lead-in to the conquest of the homeland.

Earlier, on September 27, 1944, Kuribayashi had written to his son, Tarô, and his eldest daughter, Yokô: "The island where I am will have to be taken before air raids on Tokyo can take place. To put it another way, raids will mean that your father has died with honor." Kuribayashi was convinced that as long as he and his men could hold out, Tokyo would be safe.

March 10 was Army Commemoration Day.

By this time, the second main defense line had already been broken; the Japanese had been driven into a very small area in the north of the island, and every one of the island's strategic points had fallen into enemy hands. In the bunkers in the north of the island, where every nighttime sortie only resulted in more casualties, a rumor had been circulating for a while now: "Reinforcements will come on Army Commemoration Day." There was another rumor to the effect that "everyone will be able to return to the homeland after that, on April 29, the Emperor's birthday."

In their hearts they knew it was already too late, but more than a few of the soldiers still hoped against hope. "The Imperial General Headquarters can't very well abandon an island like this, which is part of the Japanese homeland," they reasoned. "The Special Attack Force did a marvelous job of sinking the enemy battleships the other day, didn't they?"

It was on February 21 that the Special Attack Force had come to Iwo Jima's aid. The 601 Navy Air Corps, 2nd Mitate Special Attack Force, took off from Katori Air Base in Chiba Prefecture. There were nine onboard fighters (Zeros), six on-board attack planes (Tenzans), and ten on-board bombers (Suiseis). Some of these suffered mechanical problems, but the remaining twenty-one planes resolutely plowed into the American warships in the seas around Iwo Jima.

The attack started sometime after 4:00 p.m. The radio room at Katori Air Base started to receive *totsunyûden,* the transmissions announcing that a pilot was about to make his dive attack: "I will crash into a transport"; "I will target the aircraft carrier."

Meanwhile, in the navy headquarters on Iwo Jima, Rear Admiral

Rinosuke Ichimaru, the commander of the naval forces, was squeezed into the code room with Staff Officer Major Akata Kunio to monitor the Americans' radio communications. They heard alarmed voices: "Kamikaze! Kamikaze!" "How many planes?" "It's going to hit us!" At the same time, excited voices came from the wireless that linked the various installations of the Japanese on the island: "The Special Attack Force is here!" "Banzai! It's going to sink! I can see the pillar of flame!"

The 2nd Mitate Special Attack Force did a good job that day, sinking one escort aircraft carrier, inflicting serious damage on another aircraft carrier, and damaging one transport ship. This can be legitimately characterized as a significant success. During the entire Pacific War, the Special Attack Force sank only three aircraft carriers—and one of them on that day.

The radio and the newspapers gave extensive coverage to the achievements of this raid, but it was the first and last serious support that Iwo Jima was to get. According to the memoirs of Matsumoto Iwao, a noncommissioned officer of the 27th Air Corps attached to Iwo Jima headquarters, Staff Officer Akata assembled the NCOs and student officers the evening of the day when the attack took place and told them, "You'd better understand that today's attack by the Special Attack Force marks the end of any help we'll get here on Iwo Jima."

February 21 was only three days into the battle, but the central military command had no intention of expending any more planes for the sake of Iwo Jima. This was something that Kuribayashi and his staff had known all along.

AS THE FLAMES OVERRAN Tokyo on March 10, the outcome of the battle on Iwo Jima had already been decided.

Kuribayashi was starting to get reports of entire units choosing to die in suicide attacks. Although he had sternly forbidden banzai charges, the soldiers were growing physically weak as their supplies of food and water ran out. They were also surrounded by the Americans and were sure to die whether they moved forward or stayed put. Under these circumstances, it was hardly suprising that some officers decided that yelling banzai and charging to an honorable death was the better option.

Every time he received a radio message announcing a unit's intention to make a final, fatal charge, Kuribayashi would issue a stern order for them to call it off. Some units did abandon the idea, but others went through with it. The units that followed Kuribayashi's orders and canceled their plans for suicide charges left their bunkers and tried to join the forces at the Command Center. Many of them were killed by enemy fire on their way there.

The Japanese soldiers were being tormented by thirst in underground bunkers, where every day there were more corpses of their comrades. Meanwhile, just a few kilometers back from the front, the American soldiers were able to drink hot coffee and take showers. As the Japanese soldiers breathed their last with worn and creased letters from home in their breast pockets, the Americans were getting deliveries of letters from their families that had been flown over from the United States.

The Americans now regarded the Iwo Jima operation as more or less complete, and an official flag-raising ceremony was conducted on March 14. The flagstaff for this was located some 200 meters north of Mount Suribachi. As the flag was raised there, the one on top of Mount Suribachi was lowered.

A declaration of occupation by Admiral Nimitz was read at the ceremony. The man himself had already left the island for a meeting in Guam to prepare for the next campaign: the capture of Okinawa.

Lieutenant General Smith was, of course, present, near "his" marines. His eyes were full of tears as he said to Major General Graves B. Erskine, commander of the Third Division, "This is the worst yet."

But the "worst" was, in fact, far from over.

Not that far from where Lieutenant General Smith was standing, a cemetery had been built for the soldiers who had been killed on the island. Despite Nimitz's proclamation, the number of white-painted crosses there kept on growing. The Japanese soldiers did not abandon their resistance, and the fighting at the front lines was as desperate as ever. Between this day and the collapse of organized Japanese resistance that followed the death of Kuribayashi, the commander in chief, the Americans were to suffer more than two thousand more casualties.

The lines of the Japanese and American troops were now separated by as little as 50 meters. The Japanese had run out of shells and bullets and had to depend on hand grenades. They always kept an extra one for their own suicide.

By March 14, the Japanese had nine hundred men (of whom two hundred were navy personnel) left in their last stronghold in the northern end of the island. These were not the only Japanese troops left on the island. Men were still alive in bunkers in areas that the Americans had passed across, and many of them fought guerrilla style even though their units were scattered and there was no one left to lead them. Although the Americans urged them to surrender, no one complied. In parts of the island that the Americans thought they had long ago subdued, Japanese soldiers would suddenly burst out and inflict casualties on them.

The Americans started to make use of Motoyama Airfield on March 15. On March 16, Admiral Nimitz announced the end of the Iwo Jima campaign and issued a special communiqué declaring the island officially occupied. In the communiqué, Nimitz praised and thanked the marines for their unparalleled courage and self-sacrifice.

The Japanese troops were certainly not alone in fighting bravely on Iwo Jima. Looking at it impartially, one has to acknowledge that the marines' extraordinary exploits deserve to live on in history.

There were officers who continued to lead their men up until their last breath, standing in a sea of their own blood; there were men who died flinging themselves bodily onto a grenade to save their comrades. The marines may have enjoyed a significant advantage over the Japanese in terms of matériel, but the courage they showed in the face of the worst casualties since the founding of the Marine Corps was worthy of the respect and gratitude of the American people.

Nimitz's communiqué concluded with the words: "Among the Americans who served on Iwo island, uncommon valor was a common virtue."

This phrase, which extolled the capture of Iwo Jima not from the perspective of military strategy but from the perspective of individual courage and devotion to country, won the hearts of the American people. The phrase achieved overnight fame and is inscribed on the victory monument on the top of Mount Suribachi, as well as being engraved on the base of the statue of the six soldiers raising the Stars and Stripes on Suribachi in Arlington National Cemetery.

THAT SAME MARCH 16, Kuribayashi's resolve to come out and make a final all-out attack was slowly hardening.

Until this point, Kuribayashi had not allowed any units to make suicide charges, but by now the Japanese forces were completely encircled by the Americans and bottled up in a very tight space measuring around 700 meters north to south, and between 200 and 500 meters east to west. The Americans were putting pressure on the bunkers with gun- and tank fire, and Japanese casualties continued to mount. Taking this—as well as the remaining quantities of explosives, food, and water; the number of wounded; and the soldiers' physical powers of endurance—into account, Kuribayashi judged that now was the time when an all-out attack could be effective.

It was at some point after 4:00 p.m. on this day that Kuribayashi dispatched his farewell telegram to the Imperial General Headquarters.

The battle is entering its final chapter. Since the enemy's landing, the gallant fighting of the men under my command has been such that even the gods would weep. In particular, I humbly rejoice in the fact that they have continued to fight bravely though utterly empty-handed and ill-equipped against a land, sea, and air attack of a material superiority such as surpasses the imagination.

One after another they are falling to the ceaseless and ferocious attacks of the enemy. For this reason, the situation has arisen whereby I must disappoint your expectations and yield this important place to the hands of the enemy. With humility and sincerity, I offer my repeated apologies.

Our ammunition is gone and our water dried up. Now is the time for us all to make our final counterattack and fight gallantly, conscious of the Emperor's favor, not begrudging our efforts though they turn our bones to powder and pulverize our bodies.

I believe that until this island is recaptured, the Emperor's domain will be eternally insecure. I therefore swear that even when I have become a ghost I shall look forward to turning the defeat of the Imperial Army into victory.

I stand now at the beginning of the end. At the same time as revealing my inmost feelings, I pray earnestly for the unfailing victory and the security of the Empire. Farewell for all eternity.

As regards Chichi Jima and Haha Jima, I am sure that the men under my command there can completely crush any attack the enemy might make. I entrust that matter to you.

Finally, I append an inept work for your perusal below. Please forgive its clumsiness.

Postscript

> *Unable to complete this heavy task for our country*
> *Arrows and bullets all spent, so sad we fall.*
>
> *But unless I smite the enemy,*
> *My body cannot rot in the field.*
> *Yea, I shall be born again seven times*
> *And grasp the sword in my hand.*
>
> *When ugly weeds cover this island,*
> *My only thought will be the Imperial Land.*

Kuribayashi had instructed his men to live a life more agonizing than death; ordered them to wring the very last drop out of their lives. But in a battle where neither victory nor a safe return home could be hoped for, he also would not allow his men to die heroic deaths. To set down in writing how the men who had faithfully followed his orders had lived and died—something that the people in the homeland would never otherwise know—was the final duty for the commanding officer who had held the lives of more than twenty thousand men in his hands.

Kuribayashi had no way of knowing that the Imperial General Headquarters would alter his telegram, but he must have known that the phrase "empty-handed and ill-equipped" was sure to rub the higher-ups the wrong way. He must also have known that expressing grief for dying soldiers with the word "sad" was unacceptable behavior, quite unsuitable for an officer of the Imperial Army. Yes, Kuribayashi did know all that, but he wrote it nonetheless. Such was the nature of his farewell telegram.

In the early morning of March 17, Kuribayashi transmitted one more message. It was addressed to the Imperial General Headquarters, but it was actually an appeal to all his men on the island.

1. The battle is entering its final chapter.
2. On the night of the seventeenth, the whole group will execute an all-out attack and crush the enemy.
3. At midnight each unit shall attack the enemy in front of them, fighting gallantly down to the last man. The Emperor [three characters illegible] will not allow shirking.
4. I will at all times be at your head.

That everyone would die in the final all-out assault was a given, but Kuribayashi ordered one of his officers to stay alive.

That man, according to a memoir by Musashino Kikuzô, commander of the Engineering Battalion, was Major Yoshida Monzô, staff officer in charge of fortification building. Before going into combat, Kuribayashi gave him this order: "You must stay alive here on this island, then slip away from here some day and tell the citizens of Japan about the carnage here."

Yoshida did as he had been ordered. He did not die in a last charge, but lived on. First he tried to get away from the island on a raft. When that failed, he stole an American plane and attempted to fly back to Japan. That came to nothing as well. Yoshida is believed to have been killed by enemy fire in mid-May.

The final Japanese attack did not come from the Command Bunker where the enemy pressure was at its most intense, but from the Kita Engineering Corps bunker about 60 meters away, where the 145th Infantry Regiment—the core of the Iwo Jima garrison—had established its center of command. The plan called for them to unite with the remnant of the navy force under Rear Admiral Ichimaru and make the attack from there.

A memoir by First Lieutenant Tamada Takeshi that is quoted in the official history includes the following description of what happened in the Command Bunker on the night of the seventeenth before the move to the bunker of the Kita Engineering Corps.

On the evening of March 17, we burned our insignia of rank, any important documents, and our private possessions. Everyone in the headquarters cave was presented with one cup of sake and two cigarettes from the Emperor. Lieutenant General Kuribayashi grasped the pommel of his sword with his left hand and made a speech to the following effect: "Even if you have to eat grass, bite the earth, or throw yourselves on the ground, I believe that you will fight and, in so doing, find a way out of this fatal situation. With things as they are, each one of you must kill one hundred—there is nothing else for it. I believe in your devotion. Please do as I do." And on that very night the headquarters made their attack.

The passage says they "made their attack," but, in fact, no all-out attack was made that evening; all they did was move to the bunker of the Kita Engineering Corps, which was to serve as the attack base. The Americans had gotten them so tightly boxed in that they could not find any opening through which to attack.

Kuribayashi's words as recorded in this memoir are extremely heroic, but what of his appearance? The following is the testimony of Sergeant Ryûmae Shinya, who worked in the adjutant section and was one of those who made the move to the bunker of the Kita Engineering Corps that evening.

When we escaped from the Command Bunker in the dead of night on March 17, he was not energetic like the staff officers and other officers. At first glance, in fact, he looked like some old man from the countryside being led outside by his children. He was leaning on his cane, unarmed, and stood more or less in the middle of around 500 people together with the top medical officer and the head of ordnance, though the staff officers were somewhere else. That was the last I saw of our army corps commander. [From *Ogasawara Heidan no Saigo*]

Ryûmae was one of the very few survivors to have seen Kuribayashi from so close up. Takeichi Ginjirô, emeritus assistant professor of the National Defense Academy, met Ryûmae personally for research and states in his book *Iô-Tô* (*Iwo Jima*) that his testimony is extremely reliable.

Ryûmae is now dead, but, according to someone he spoke to before his death, he said, "His Lordship Kuribayashi had always been hale and hearty, but by then he was completely different: emaciated and with an expression of total exhaustion on his face."

In few of the works written about the battle of Iwo Jima does one find any mention of Kuribayashi having shown any sign of weakness. Only Takeichi Ginjirô in *Iô-Tô* says that "He revealed a degree of spiritual frailty at the final stage when the annihilation of his men was imminent"; and that "The responsibility of forcing the men under his command to die in so cruel a battle unsettled his mind." In all the other texts he is portrayed as a dauntless leader from first to last.

If we extrapolate from the image of Kuribayashi that emerges from his interactions with his men, the letters he wrote to his family, his war-lesson telegrams, and his farewell telegram, it does not seem impossible that he might have plunged into sudden despondency at the final stage.

What broke Kuribayashi's spirit?

As Professor Takeichi points out, one likely cause was having to force the men under his command to take part in so merciless a battle. Kuribayashi was the kind of man incapable of regarding the soldiers he commanded—even the common soldiers whom he had never met—as mere pawns to be used to advance the cause of war. The sight of the weak, emaciated, and ghostlike soldiers dying in such numbers as they faced the terrifying intensity of the American assault on one hand, while suffering from hunger and thirst on the other, seems to have been a crushing blow for Kuribayashi.

Another factor could well have been him finding out that Tokyo had been subjected to indiscriminate strategic bombing on an unprecedented scale.

Kuribayashi is likely to have heard about the great air raid on Tokyo by this stage. He was still in communication with the Imperial General Headquarters and was able to receive radio broadcasts. Radio Tokyo (Japan Broadcasting Corporation Overseas Department) was making propaganda broadcasts aimed at the American troops in Asia and the Pacific region. Directly after the raid on Tokyo, it reported that the Japanese capital had been the victim of indiscriminate bombing from the air and voiced strong criticism of the United States, pointing out that the fire set off by the incendiaries had caused tremendous damage, the bulk of it being borne by unarmed civilians. The horrors Kuribayashi heard about certainly went beyond anything he could have imagined.

One thing that had made Kuribayashi's men stand firm through the dreadful horrors of a battle they were doomed to lose was their desire to protect Japanese civilians from the horrors of air raids. They hoped that, while they were delaying the American invasion of the homeland, negotiations to end the war would get under way. For Kuribayashi, who always expected Japan to be defeated, that was the only thing that could give meaning to his sacrificing the lives of the men under his command.

Of all the letters Kuribayashi sent to his family, only four do not touch on the subject of air raids against the Japanese mainland. He urges them to be careful, lectures them about taking shelter, repeats that he and all the other fathers are fighting on Iwo Jima so that the people back on the mainland will be spared from air raids. The thought that he was going to lay down his life in Iwo Jima to protect his wife and children in Tokyo probably sustained Kuribayashi, just as it did the other officers and men.

But then Tokyo was ravaged by fire, and ordinary civilians were killed. When he heard the news, Kuribayashi's despair and sense of failure must have been tremendous. He did not even know if his wife and children were alive. They were, in fact, safe and sound—but he had no way of knowing that.

NONETHELESS, HE DID NOT lose the will to fight.

After postponing the attack on the night of the seventeenth, Kuribayashi spent a further eight days waiting patiently for the right moment for an all-out attack. The other survivors surely admired Kuribayashi, who, though exhausted and aged beyond his years, still refused to abandon his policy of endurance, and forbade any premature assault. Or were some of them fed up? Now that they were trapped, many of his men must have just wanted to get their charge over and done with as soon as possible. They had, after all, drunk their parting toasts to one another on the seventeenth.

It can certainly be argued that given the realities of the situation—the mainland devastated by B-29s and ordinary civilians engulfed in the horrors of war—the main reason to defend Iwo Jima so doggedly had now vanished. On the other hand, were the island to be completely conquered, bigger American units could come ashore to give the runways a proper overhaul. Clearly that would only make the air raids on the mainland worse.

Kuribayashi remained firm, and his commitment to holding out to the end, in an effort to reduce the damage wrought by air raids on the mainland, never wavered. Nor had he abandoned the notion that making the enemy bleed would help peace negotiations to proceed on more favorable terms.

I suspect that there was a further reason why Kuribayashi did not make a banzai charge, no matter how bad things got.

The victim of a series of policy changes in the overall strategy of the military central command, Iwo Jima ended up having to face the enemy all by itself.

Initially the Imperial General Headquarters had regarded Iwo Jima as important. Why else would they send twenty thousand soldiers to the place? But as the Americans' invasion got nearer, the island was suddenly labeled worthless and cut off. The Japanese forces on Iwo Jima ended up having to fight with almost no support from the air force or the navy. *Daihonei Rikugunbu 10 Shôwa nijû-nen hachi-gatsu made* ("Imperial General Headquarters Army Section, Volume 10: Up to August 1945") in the *Senshisôsho* official history produced by the Military History Department of the National Institute for Defense describes how the Imperial General Headquarters took the news of the fall of Iwo Jima.

> The military central command had foreseen the loss of Iwo Jima to some degree. They praised the gallant fighting of the defense garrison and admired the way Kuribayashi had exercised his command, but did not display any very marked reaction.

They "had foreseen the loss of Iwo Jima to some degree" so they "did not display any very marked reaction." How casually the war leaders were prepared to give up on twenty thousand lives!

The Imperial General Headquarters ran through a series of stopgap policies that had no relation to reality, and then, when they got deadlocked and had nowhere to go, they wrote places off as hopeless. The result was soldiers going to their deaths in banzai charges that they themselves knew to be almost ineffectual in places the headquarters had decided to abandon, while the generals killed themselves by committing hara-kiri. This is what happened on Attu and Talau, and at Saipan and Guam. My guess is that Kuribayashi did not want to be party to the fraud of calling such a death by the meretricious name of *gyokusai*, "honorable death"—a combination of the ideograms for "beautiful jewel" and "pulverize"—or of using the samurai aesthetic to conceal mistaken projections and foolhardy strategies.

Kuribayashi was a rationalist, and he loved the soldiers who served under him. If they were in a battle from which they could not return alive, then the least he could do was give them a "worthwhile death," and that is why his policy of not allowing banzai charges stayed consistent from first to last.

Kuribayashi was a warrior who respected the realities, if not the aesthetic conventions of war, and the extreme campaign that he waged on Iwo Jima and the manner in which he chose to die showed just how empty the values professed by the Japanese military establishment were.

The American encirclement relaxed a little around the nineteenth. Kuribayashi took his time examining the situation, and on the evening of the twenty-fourth judged that the siege had loosened sufficiently to provide a window for the attack.

According to Ôyama Jun, one of the survivors, Kuribayashi delivered a speech before the attack on the night of March 25.

> Even if I should perish before you in the battle, the glorious exploits that you have carried out will never be forgotten. Japan may now be losing this battle, but the people of Japan are burning at your loyalty and your patriotism; they are praising your glorious deeds; and the day will come when they offer silent prayers for your ghosts. Be easy in your minds and sacrifice yourself for your country.*

* From Okada Masukichi, "Iô-Jima ni Kakeru Shôgai" ("Lives on the Line at Iwo Jima"), *Maru*, June 1959.

"I will at all times be at your head," Kuribayashi had said in the appeal telegraphed to all the surviving men, and, true to his word, Kuribayashi took up his position at the head of around four hundred men from the army and the navy. They rose above despair and summoned up their last reserves of willpower.

Normally during a final all-out charge, the commanding officer would commit hara-kiri behind the lines. But this was yet another convention that Kuribayashi ignored. A document related to practical training on Iwo Jima from the Ground Self-Defense Force Officer School says: "There is no other example in the history of the Japanese army where a division commander (army corps commander) led the charge himself. This all-out counterattack is highly unusual."

Led by Kuribayashi, the group moved south along the coast down toward Mount Suribachi and fell upon an encampment of marines and army air corps just after five o'clock on the morning of the twenty-sixth. The Americans, who were confident that organized resistance by the Japanese was long over, fell into panic. After a furious fight at close quarters lasting for around three hours, the Japanese had inflicted 170 casualties on the Americans. The surviving Japanese soldiers then made a charge onto Motoyama and Chidori Airfields, where the majority of them were killed.

The Americans did not know that Kuribayashi had led this attack. It was nothing like a banzai charge. The Japanese soldiers made a silent and well-organized attack that took the Americans by surprise and caused them unexpected damage. The entry on "Iwo Jima" in the *United States Marine Corps History* evaluates it thus: "The Japanese attack on the early morning of March 26 was not a *banzai* charge, but an excellent plan aiming to cause maximum confusion and destruction."

At some point Kuribayashi was seriously wounded in his right thigh, but still pushed on, carried on the back of a first sergeant attached to the headquarters. He is thought to have died either from loss of blood or to have taken his own life with a pistol shot. No one survived who witnessed the last moments of this commander who fought side by side with his men until his own death.

THE MORNING KURIBAYASHI DIED, the 77th Infantry Division of the U.S. Army landed on the Kerama Islands of Okinawa, 1,380 kilometers away from Iwo Jima. The civilians were drawn into the battle, and this marked the start of the Battle of Okinawa, which eventually produced so many—some say one hundred thousand—civilian casualties.

Yoshii was forty years old when her husband lost his life on Iwo Jima. A housewife ever since her marriage at the age of nineteen, she was suddenly responsible for earning the family livelihood while also taking care of her three children.

Takako, Kuribayashi's second daughter, can remember her mother out in the streets of Nagano just after the war, where her family home was located, selling dried cuttlefish she'd somehow managed to get her hands on. After the family returned to Tokyo, Yoshii rented a small place near Nagano station, where she sold wooden clogs and other footwear.

She later worked as an insurance saleswoman, and eventually got a job as live-in matron at the staff dormitory of a spinning company in Tokyo's Setagaya Ward. Takako lived in the dormitory building with her mother until leaving high school. The two women then lived in a one-room apartment, sharing cooking and toilet facilities with the other residents. When relatives of soldiers who had died on Iwo Jima visited them to borrow money, Yoshii would hand over as much as she could with an apology: "I'm afraid this is all that we've got. . . ."

"My mother had been brought up as a lady, and even after getting married she had been taken care of by my father. She had never worked in her life before, but she still managed to raise us during the terrible times after the war by doing things like selling cuttlefish out on the street. And more than that, she sent not just my elder brother, but me, a girl, to university."

Kuribayashi never ordered his wife to live as a proper soldier's wife, taking care not to soil her husband's good name after he was gone. Indeed, he seems to have said quite the opposite in his letters from Iwo Jima. In one dated September 4, 1944, he tells her that he's depending on her to bring up the children and continues: "From now on, don't worry about things like keeping up appearances or what other people say about you. What's important is for you to believe in yourself and go your own way."

A lieutenant general, Kuribayashi was posthumously promoted to full general in recognition of his heroic defense of Iwo Jima. Yoshii was therefore supposed to live with the pride proper to the wife of a general. But in her case that did not mean guarding the family name and passing the exploits of her husband down to her children and her children's children. That was not what her husband wanted from her.

Other people and appearances don't matter, believe in yourself and live your way. Confront harsh reality head-on, and be strong together with your children. That was what Kuribayashi asked his wife to do when he knew that he would no longer be able to take care of his family. And Yoshii rose to the challenge, living through the postwar years with a strength that had nothing to do with worldly appearances or the opinions of other people.

One day after the children had grown up and left home, and she was able to live a less fraught existence, Yoshii had a dream. Her husband, whom she knew to be dead, stood grinning in the entryway of their house dressed in his army uniform. When she appeared startled, he said gently, "I just got back now."

Ah, she thought, so you did come back to me after all. Happiness flooded her heart—and then she woke up. Even after she realized that it was a dream, the joy remained undimmed. Her husband had looked genuinely happy.

Very soon after that came the news that, after twenty-three years, the United States would be returning the Ogasawara Islands to Japan.

—

I VISITED MATSUSHIRO-MACHI, Kuribayashi's hometown in Nagano, in the early summer of 2004.

The erstwhile castle town of Sanada Jûmangoku, Matsushiro-Machi was also the birthplace of Sakuma Shôzan, a leading progressive from the last years of the Tokugawa regime. The house where Kuribayashi was born is located in a quiet fold of a hill a little to the south of the center near the historic sights of Sanada's residence and the Matsushiro Civil and Military School. As you walk up a gentle incline, the first thing you see is an old stone storehouse, then, beyond that, there stands an old two-story house with a tiled roof and white plaster walls. The house dates from the early Showa period, and the garden is full of white and pink peonies.

I was welcomed by Kuribayashi Naotaka, the present head of the family. Naotaka is the grandson of Kuribayashi's elder brother, Yoshima. He was born in 1945, after Kuribayashi's death, and is the principal of a junior high school.

The Kuribayashis are an old family. They have lived here since the Warring States period (1467–1568), when they were "country samurai" administering a barrier station for the Sanada clan. A country samurai is a samurai who does not move his abode to the castle town of his lord, but stays and farms in his own home place.

In the Tokugawa period (1600–1868), the Kuribayashis became clansmen of the Matsushiro clan, and in the Meiji period (1868–1912), they invested in the silk-reeling industry and the banking business, but failed in both due to "samurai business methods" (an aristocratic tendency to regard commerce as beneath one). Their house burned to the ground in both 1868 and 1881. In 1891 his parents were working hard to rebuild the place when Kuribayashi was born.

Yoshima's eldest son Sunao wrote an unpublished essay about his uncle's youth. Entitled "The Young Days of Kuribayashi Tadamichi," the handwritten manuscript is preserved in the house. In it we learn that Kuribayashi's father, Tsurujirô, engaged in the lumber and civil engineering businesses, while his mother, Moto, ran the farm with the servants. The parents were always busy, and from an early age the children used to help with domestic tasks like scrubbing the corridors and taking care of the garden. Despite being born into a "good" family in the provinces, Kuribayashi's upbringing was simple and hardworking, and had nothing to do with luxury.

Kuribayashi progressed from Matsushiro Higher Elementary School to Nagano Middle School (currently Nagano High School). His grades were excellent and his English was particularly good—he is even said to have dreamed of becoming a roving foreign correspondent. According to anecdote, while on Iwo Jima he told the reporter Shishikura Tsunetaka that he had thought about becoming a journalist himself. And indeed, he sat the entrance examination not just for the Military Academy, but also sat and passed that for Shanhai Tôa Dôbun Shoin, a prestigious college for Japanese students in Shanghai, China. Kuribayashi was unsure which to choose, but finally decided to go to the Military Academy on the advice of his teacher.

After that he took the typical path of the elite officer, attending the Army War College and going abroad to study. But he never worked in the Imperial General Headquarters, never had any involvement with politics, and was not interested in the jockeying for position that went on between the different army factions.

His progress up the ranks was not especially fast for someone who had been honored with a saber from the emperor on graduation, and his appointments to major general and lieutenant general were both a good six months behind his fastest contemporaries at college. His career was surprisingly unglamorous—he spent a long time in a post where he was responsible for the army's cavalry horses—and nothing really stands out until he was appointed commander in chief on Iwo Jima.

Iwo Jima was not just a remote place; you were unlikely to make it back home alive. Many other generals came up with excuses to wriggle out of being sent there and, in a sense, Kuribayashi was the only one foolishly honest enough to say yes. Once he had accepted, he fulfilled his duty heroically, as I hope this book shows. In matters of war, Kuribayashi was a rationalist, but when it came to his life philosophy, he had an almost naive conviction that a soldier's duty was to go out to the front lines and put himself in harm's way.

An examination of Kuribayashi's experiences on Iwo Jima reveals such a gulf between the men who risked their lives on the front and the top brass who were responsible for overall direction of the war that one is reluctant to apply the word "soldier" to both groups. The staff officers ensconced in the safety of the Imperial General Headquarters did not even try to find out how the war was really progressing, but just drew lines on a map and declared: "Such-and-such place must be defended to the death." Kuribayashi was on the receiving end of those orders, and he was the one who went out to an isolated and unsupported battle zone.

In February 1994, the first Japanese emperor to set foot on Iwo Jima composed a poem there.

> *The men who fought heart and soul,*
> *Still sleep beneath the ground*
> *On this sad isle.*

The central command may have written the island off, but Kuribayashi's twenty thousand plus men were still determined to do their duty as best they could and put up a formidable fight. Each and every one of them truly "fought heart and soul."

The emperor's poem and Kuribayashi's death poem in his farewell telegram are linked by a common word: "sad," the very word that the Imperial General Headquarters chose to alter, changing "so sad we fall" to "mortified we fall."

It is no coincidence. After the passage of forty-nine years, the emperor of a new and different epoch acknowledged Kuribayashi's fine poem. And he did it on the sands of Iwo Jima, the very place where Kuribayashi wrote about the sadness of the soldiers going to their deaths.

THE KURIBAYASHI FAMILY GRAVE stands in Takitanzan Meitokuji Temple not far from the house where Kuribayashi was born. Meitokuji is an ancient temple, and generation after generation of Kuribayashis have served as parish representatives.

Naotaka took me to the cemetery. After we passed through the quiet temple precincts, the cemetery spread out before us ringed by the fresh foliage of trees. The mountain onto which the cemetery backs is Mount Minakami, which contains the ruins of the Matsushiro Imperial Headquarters.

The Matsushiro Imperial Headquarters is an underground bunker complex. It was built to accommodate the Imperial General Headquarters, the Imperial family, government ministries and agencies, and the national broadcaster, all of whom were to move out of Tokyo before the decisive battle for the homeland. Construction began in November 1944 at Mount Zô and Mount Maizuru as well as Minakami and continued without a single day's pause until August 15, 1945.

At exactly the same time Kuribayashi was working frantically to dig his underground bunkers on Iwo Jima, another large-scale bunker complex was being excavated in the very place where he had been born and raised. Both were expected to save the nation.

The plan to move Imperial General Headquarters to Matsushiro was top secret. The words "Imperial General Headquarters" do not appear anywhere on the original blueprints; instead, the facility is called "Matsushiro Storage Space." Kuribayashi, however, seems to have known what was going on, as this passage from his November 28, 1944, letter to his elder brother, Yoshima, suggests: "As regards the military facility at Mount Minakami, they are starting to implement a plan, which was pending until recently. I think it extremely unlikely that the enemy will bomb the area."

Standing in front of Kuribayashi's grave, you can see Mount Minakami off to the right. Peaceful and dripping with lush green, it is hard to believe that within its womb is a vast, dark cave fathered by war.

His grave is simple: an ordinary rectangular upright stone on which the words "The Grave of General Kuribayashi Tadamichi" are carved. There is also a single sentence from a letter dated January 12, 1945, that I had just been allowed to read: the last letter he sent to his brother Yoshima in the house where he had been born: "Finally, should the worst come to the worst, I don't mind where my grave is located. A single stone shaft with the words 'The Grave of Lieutenant General Kuribayashi Tadamachi' is all I need."

There was a holder for name cards beside the grave. It contained two cards. The families of the men who lost their lives on Iwo Jima still come to pay their respects. Few of them visit the Kuribayashi house, but they all offer incense and prayer. The soldiers on Iwo Jima came from all over Japan, and the addresses on the two cards were both from Kanagawa Prefecture near Tokyo.

The present head of the Kuribayashi family, whose great-uncle was an illustrious general, picked up the cards, brushed a thin film of dust off them with his finger, and tucked them neatly into his breast pocket.

ACKNOWLEDGMENTS

I visited Tarô, Kuribayashi Tadamichi's son, in the autumn of 2003 for the simple reason that a single phrase in one of the letters from Iwo Jima really spoke to me. My research for this book dates from when Tarô welcomed me, a complete stranger, with such warmth, and let me handle and read the letters he had so carefully preserved. Tarô passed away on March 24, 2005, at the age of eighty. I am sorry that he was unable to read the completed book.

I interviewed Tarô's younger sister, Shindô Takako, several times from late 2003 to early 2004. Takako, who sang me "The Moon in the Rain" and "The Sky of Home," also passed on, about six months after that, at the age of sixty-nine. They both provided me with precious information and encouraged me in my writing. I thank them from my heart.

I belong to a generation ignorant of war. I was only able to write about this poorly documented battle thanks to the numerous people who helped me with my research, including the Association of Iwo Jima, the survivors who wrote accounts of their experiences, and professional historians of Iwo Jima. I take this opportunity to thank you all very much.

Last of all, speaking as one of the following generation, I would like to express my respect and gratitude for everyone who took part in the war and endured indescribable hardships before dying far away from their homes.

LIST OF INTERVIEWEES

Kuribayashi Tarô; Kuribayashi Fumiko; Kuribayashi Naotaka; Kuribayashi Hideko; Kuribayashi Kaoru; Kuribayashi Toshinori; Kuribayashi Kazuko; Kuribayashi Matsue; Shindô Takako; Sadaoka Nobuyoshi; Ôkoshi Harunori; Yamagiwa Yoshikazu; Egawa Mitsue; Egawa Jun; Kobayashi Michiko; Tanaka Kenichi; Fushiwara Takahiro; Shishikura Madoka; Shishikura Eiko; Nozu Naoko; Suwabe Junichirô; Nakamura Tadanori; Tamura Akiko.

BIBLIOGRAPHY

Bôeichô Bôeikenshûjo Senshishitsu. *Senshisôsho Chûbu Taiheyô Rikugun Sakusen 2 Periryû• Angauru• Iô-Jima.* Asagumo Shimbunsha

——. *Senshisôsho Daihonei Rikugunbu 10 Shôwa nijû-nen hachi-gatsu made.* Asagumo Shimbunsha

——. *Senshisôsho Daihonei Kaigunbu/Rengô Kantai 7 Sensô Saishûki.* Asagumo Shimbunsha

Rikusenshi Kenkyû Fukyûkai Hen. *Rikusenshishû 15 Dainijisekaitaisen-shi Iô-Jima Sakusen.* Hara Shobô

Iô-Jima Kyôkai Kaihô, Nos. 1–35. Iô-Jima Kyôkai

Kaikô, March 1976–December 2003. Kaikôsha

Takeichi Ginjrô. *Iô-Tô Kyokugen no Senjô ni Kizamareta Nihonjin no Tamashii.* Ômura Shoten

Funasaka Hiroshi. *Iô-Jima Aa! Kuribayashi Heidan.* Kôdansha

Kojima Noboru. *Shôgun Totsugeki seri Iô-Jima Senki.* Bungei Shunjû

Ishii Shûji. *Nanpô Horyo Sôsho Iô-Tô ni Ikiru.* Kokusho kankô kai

Ogasawara Senyûkai Hen. *Ogasawara Heidan no Saigo.* Hara Shobô

Horie Yoshitaka. *Tôkon Iô-Tô.* Kôbunsha, 1965.

Andô Tomiji. *Aa Iô-Jima.* Kawade Shobô

Tada Minoru. *Nanimo Kataranakatta Seishun.* Mikasa Shobô.

Kuribayashi Tadamichi. *Gyokusai Sôshikikan no Etegami.* Edited by Yoshida Tsuyuko. Shôgakukan Bunko

Nimitz, C. W., and E. B. Potter. *The Great Sea War: The Story of Naval Action in World War II.* Translated by Sanematsu Yuzuru and Tominaga Kengo. Kôbunsha

Smith, Holland M., and Percy Finch. *Coral and Brass.* Zenger Publishers

Ross, Bill D. *Iwo Jima: Legacy of Valor.* Translation supervised by Minato Kazuo. Yomiuri Shimbunsha

Newcomb, Richard F. *Iwo Jima.* Translated by Tanaka Itaru. Kôjinsha NF Bunko

Bradley, J., with Ron Powers. *Flags of Our Fathers.* Translated by Shimada Sanzô. Bunshun Bunko

Moriyama Kôhei. *Nihon no Senreki Iô-Jima no Kessen.* Gakken M Bunko

Nakamura Eiju, ed. *Iô-Jima Mura wa Kieta, Senzen no Rekishi o Tadoru.* Iô-Jima Senzenshi Kankôkai

Hashimoto Mamoru et al. *Iô-Tô Kessen.* Kôjinsha NF Bunko

Handô Kazutoshi. *Senshi no Isho.* Bunshun Bunko

Kawazu Yukihide. *America Kaiheitai no Taiheiyô Jôriku Sakusen Ge.* Ariadone Kikaku

Kerr, E. Bartlett. *Flames over Tokyo: The U.S. Army Air Force's Incendiary Campaign Against Japan, 1944–1945.* Translated by Ôtani Isao. Kôjinsha NF Bunko

Marshall, Chester. *B-29 Super Fortress (Warbird History).* Translated by Takaki Kôji. Neko Publishing

Saotome Katsumoto. *Tokyo Daikûshû.* Iwanami Shinsho

Takagi Sôkichi. *Taiheiyô Kaisenshi* (Kaiteiban). Iwanami Shinsho

Hayashi Saburô. *Taiheiyô Sensô Rikusen Gaishi.* Iwanami Shinsho

Nonaka Ikujirô. *America Kaiheitai.* Chûkô Shinsho

Kojima Noboru. *Taiheiyô Sensô,* Jô/Ge. Chûkô Bunko

Taiheiyô Sensô Kenkyûkai. *Zusetsu Taiheiyô Sensô.* Edited by Ikeda Kiyoshi. Kawade Shobô Shinsha

Hori Eizô. *Daihonei Sanbô no Jôhô Senki.* Bunshun Bunko

Kido Kôichi Nikki. Tôkyô Daigaku Shuppan Kai

Hara Takeshi and Yasuoka Akio, eds. *Nihon Rikukaigun Jiten.* Shin-Jinbutsuôraisha

Taiheiyô Sensô Kenkyûkai. *Nihon Rikugun ga yoku Wakaru Jiten.* PHP Bunko

Kitamuro Tsunenobu. *Senji Yôgo no Kiso Chishiki.* Kôjinsha NF Bunko

Nihon Rikugun Heiki Shû. K K World Photo Press

Sayama Jirô. *Taihô Nyûmon.* Kôjinsha NF Bunko

Asahi Shimbun Shukusatsu Ban, June 1944–August 1945

Yomiuri Shimbun (*Yomiuri Hôchi*) Shukusatsu Ban, June 1944–August 1945

Mainichi Shimbun Shukusatsu Ban, June 1944–August 1945

New York Times, February–March 1945

Time, March 5, 1945

Kuribayashi Sunao. *Wakaki Hi no Kuribayashi Tadamichi*

KUMIKO KAKEHASHI was born in 1961 in Kumamoto Prefecture. After graduating from Hokkaido University, she worked as a freelance writer producing numerous interviews and articles for newspapers and magazines. She is one of the regular contributors of human interest–based reportage to the "Gendai no Shôzô" ("Present-day Portraits") section in *AERA* magazine. She also edits books and was in charge of compiling Yoshimoto Takaaki's *Hikikomore* and *Chôrenairon* (Daiwashobô). This is her first book.